SCOTLAND VS ENGLAND

Also by Ian Black

SCOTLAND VS ENGLAND

WHAT WILL THEY DO WITHOUT US?

Ian Black

BLACK & WHITE PUBLISHING

First published 2014
by Black & White Publishing Ltd
29 Ocean Drive, Edinburgh EH6 6JL

1 3 5 7 9 10 8 6 4 2   14 15 16 17

ISBN   978 1 84502 927 2

A CIP catalogue record for this book is available from the British Library.

Typeset by RefineCatch Limited, Bungay, Suffolk
Printed and bound by Grafica Veneta S. p. A., Italy

For my country, my clan and my comrades in arms

Contents

Introduction

Back in 2007 I wrote: 'Now that we have our own parliament and that English folk are beginning to realise that we are getting a bit difficult to patronise, watch out for the wave of resentment, ungrateful brats that we are. And, if we do vote for the SNP and independence, this wave will become a veritable tsunami.'

Who was right?

Welcome to Project Fear ... and to more pro-Independence and anti No-voters jokes and tales than you can shake a stick at.

'Thrawn' is not an English word, but it is a Scottish attitude, stubborn to the power of ten. Tell us 'no', would they?

There was a recent poll in England that found that 68% of English people want their own parliament. Most people in Scotland think that the English folk already have their own parliament.

We have been consistently lied to for 300-odd years, but are we downhearted? No. We have become accustomed to the lies piled upon lies, particularly recently. Mr Osborne seems to have taken a tip from

Talleyrand, the renowned French conniving, lying bastard, who said: 'Diplomacy is the art of saying "nice doggie!" till you can find a bigger stick.'

Talleyrand also said, 'A diplomat who says "yes" means "maybe", a diplomat who says "maybe" means "no", and a diplomat who says "no" is no diplomat.' Mr Osborne does not seem to have absorbed these particular *mots non justes*.

As the somewhat arrogant MP said to the Scot, 'Take away your generosity to each other and the rest of the world, your reputation for honesty, your friendliness, your beautiful scenery with its lochs, mountains and heather, your whisky, your tartan, and what have you got?'

Said the Scot, 'England.'

And then there were the two English ladies who were discussing their holiday plans in a tea shop. At the next table sat a nice little Scots lady.

'We're planning a lovely holiday in Devon this year,' said the first English lady.

'Oh! You shouldn't do that,' said her friend. 'There are hordes of Scots there. It'll be awful!'

'Dear me!' her friend replied. 'And where will you be going?'

'Salisbury.'

'But Salisbury is simply crawling with Scots!' the first lady objected.

Introduction

At this point the dear little Scots lady could hold her tongue no longer. 'Why don't ye both go tae hell?' she suggested. 'There'll be no Scots there.'

This book explains that the new Scots currency will be the dreichma, or possibly the punt, though apparently all of the punts are in south-east England rescuing people who built houses on flood plains. See *Schadenfreude?* See me?

I apologise for occasional mutterings of 'durty English bastards' as I wrote this. The great majority of English folk are not dirty, at least by their standards, and the real filth resides in Westminster, which has more plots than there are allotments in Scotland.

Incidentally, what goes 'putt' and what goes 'putt, putt, putt, putt'?

A Scottish golfer and an English golfer at St Andrews.

And there's more. Read on.

1
Just Vote Yes, OK?

In which questions of individual and collective liberty are discussed, No-voters are dissed and no insults at all are offered to those tubes at Westminster and the bastard Tories. It should be pointed out that 'no-hoper' and 'No-voter' are interchangeable in this chapter.

'He who would trade liberty for some imagined security deserves neither liberty nor security.'
Benjamin Franklin

Benjamin also said the following:
'Did not strong connections draw me elsewhere, I believe Scotland is the country I should choose to end my days in.'
You would have been made welcome, Benjamin.

What happens to a girl who goes out with a no-hoper for an evening?
Nothing.

Every No-voter has a mind like a sprung steel trap –
always closed.

A penny saved is a government oversight.

Yes-voters live longer than No-voters, but No-voters
are a lot more willing to die.

Why do No-voters not stare out of the window in the
morning?
    Because then they would have nothing to do in the
afternoon.

Osborne   pronouncement: 'There's   one   major
advantage in being poor. It's very inexpensive.'

Is Gideon's wife dissatisfied with his body?
    A tiny part of him says yes.

Mrs   Frances   Osborne   went   for   relationship
counselling, and the counsellor told her that she
needed to be more open with Gideon about what she
wanted in bed.
    Apparently 'someone else' wasn't an acceptable
answer.

After deep and complex theorising and discussion (OK, a few minutes in the pub), the author of this volume and Willie McIlvanney, a genuinely deep and complex thinker (and an infinitely better author), have come up with these thoughts on the infinite variables surrounding the question of the referendum vote:

If we vote Yes there is some possibility that we might be fucked.

If we vote No we are certainly going to be fucked.

I may have put in the sweary words, as Willie, one of life's gentlemen, is as suave as fuck.

And Willie also has this to say about this wee place that we call home:

'There is a deeply ingrained tradition in Scotland that we will not finally judge one another by material standards. A country as poor as we have been for so long has at least learnt that there are more important measures of a human being than the financial – more significant assessments of a nation than the stock market. We have a humane tradition to uphold second to that of no other nation.'

Surviving the Shipwreck (1991)

How many No-voters does it take to stop a train?

Not enough.

A sensible bloke named Peter went to his doctor after a long illness. The doctor, after a lengthy examination, sighed, looked Peter in the eye and said, 'I've some bad news for you, Peter . . . you have cancer and it can't be cured. I'd give you two weeks to a month.'

Peter, shocked and saddened by the news, but of solid character, managed to compose himself and walk from the doctor's office into the waiting room.

There he saw his son, who had been waiting. Peter said, 'Son, we Scots celebrate when things are good and celebrate when things don't go so well. In this case, things aren't so well. I have cancer and I've been given a short time to live. Let's head for the pub and have a few pints.'

After three or four pints the two were feeling a little less sombre and a little less sober. There were some laughs and more beers. They were eventually approached by some of Peter's business acquaintances, Tories and No-voters to a man, who asked what the two were celebrating. Peter told them that Scottish Republicans celebrate the good and the bad and went on to tell them that they were drinking to his impending end. He told them, 'I've only got a few weeks to live as I have been diagnosed with AIDS.' They gave Peter their somewhat insincere condolences and slunk off to find out who was getting his job.

After they left, Peter's son leaned over and

whispered, 'Dad, I thought you said that you were dying from cancer. You just told those guys that you were dying from AIDS.'

Peter said, 'I am dying from cancer, son, I just don't want any of those no-hoper fucking losers bothering your mammy after I'm gone.'

Examination to Become a No-voter
PART I (WRITTEN)

INSTRUCTIONS TO CANDIDATES

(a) Do not attempt to answer more than one question at a time.
(b) Do not attempt to write on both sides of the paper at the same time.
(c) On no account attempt Question 3.
(d) Slide rules OK.

NB. Candidates caught cheating will be given extra marks for initiative. All candidates are requested to use separate answer books.

Time allowed: 6 weeks.

1. Who won the Second World War? Who came second?
2. Explain in one sentence Einstein's Theory of Relativity OR write your name in block capitals.

3. What is the number of this question?

4. Name the odd man out: the Chief Rabbi, the Pope, Jack the Ripper, the Archbishop of Canterbury.

5. At the All-Scotland Sheepdog Trials of 2013, how many sheepdogs were found guilty?

6. At what time is the nine o'clock news broadcast?

7. Spell each of the following words: DOG, CAT, PIG.

8. Write a tongue-twister three times quickly.

9. There have been six kings of England named George. The latest was George the Sixth – name the other five.

10. Quote four lines from any poem written in the English language or from any other poem written in the English language.

NB. This is the Honours paper – there is a special pass version for Maybes.

PART II (PRACTICAL)

Leave the examination hall and persuade the first passer-by you meet to accompany you through life, using irony, should you know what that means, where necessary.

Scotland vs England

Two Aberdeen rugby teams, one made up of No-voters and one of Yes-voters, fly in and charter an open-top double-decker at Edinburgh airport to get them to a weekend tournament in Edinburgh. The Yes-voters are in the bottom of the bus, and the No-hopers on top. The team down below is whooping it up and having a great time when one of them realises he's not hearing anything from the guys upstairs. He decides to go up and investigate. When he reaches the top, he finds all the No-voters frozen in fear, staring straight ahead at the road and clutching the seats in front of them. The Yes-voter says, 'What's going on up here? We're having a great time downstairs.'

One of the No-hopers says, 'Aye, but you've got a driver!'

2
The Case for Us

Scotland no longer sends the great ships seawards in pride, as they have gone to deeper channels and cheaper labour, and we are no longer the industrial giant that we were when Glasgow boasted of being the Second City of the Empire, but Scotland is probably known worldwide more than it ever was and, as any Tartan Army footsoldier will tell you, the image is a positive one.

Did you know that native Scots or those descended directly from them have been the recipients of 11% of all the Nobel Prizes that have ever been awarded? We invented the steam engine, the bicycle, tarmacadam roads, the telephone, television, the transistor, the motion picture, penicillin, electromagnetics, radar, insulin, calculus and a whole raft of other stuff, including proper sweaters, shortbread and the passing game at football.

The Victorian historian James Anthony Froude noted, 'No people so few in number have scored so deep a mark in the world's history as the Scots have done.' It is not just about haggis and kilts, important though both are.

In 1994, Julia Roberts said, when asked if she'd like some haggis, 'I'd rather starve,' so she might be the exception that proves the rule, as the collecting of the honest, sonsie (and cheaper) bits of sheep and then boiling them in its stomach is proving more successful than it has ever been. Burns Suppers are a growth industry all over the world and, as we all know, once you have tasted haggis, one isn't enough. They're addictive, a bit like caramel wafers and macaroon bars, and other things that nobody else in the world makes, like plain bread and mutton pies. And do we not make the most tooth-rotting but delicious sweeties you can buy anywhere?

As for kilts, if you were setting out to buy a brand, the kilt would cost you more than Bill Gates has ever made. It is a stoater of an image and a babe magnet of enormous pulling force abroad, though I am sure that that isn't the reason that the proportion of people, and not just the Tartan Army, wearing the kilt abroad has risen so dramatically. I can remember a kilt-wearer being a figure of fun and a genuine rarity. Not any more. Anyone who pokes fun at a kiltie caul bum these days is likely to remember doing so, and not for positive reasons.

Another thing that no one else in the world can claim is Scotch whisky. We make the best whisky there is, thousands of different kinds, and the world has recognised this by buying it in all its different presentations, as well as forming clubs and associations, thousands of them too, to share its deep pleasures. Where else can you find a drink that tastes of, in no particular order, peat, lemons, oranges, cinnamon, green fruits, cloves, vanilla, toffee, sultanas and sea fog? And that is just one of them.

Also, of course, we have the best water in the world, extremely suitable for insertion into whisky, as well as for making it. God and/or complex chemical processes made the water, but I love thinking of the Scottish guy at Highland Spring, or wherever, saying to himself, 'We need something that is cheaper than dirt and that we've got too much of, and then we need to sell it at a profit. I know, water. Eureka! Bob's your uncle and Fanny's your auntie.' Now the world is buying our water in ever-increasing quantities. And we are also making electricity with it. Brilliant idea.

As it does fall from the sky in such industrial volumes, we have also, as a certain Mr Macintosh might demonstrate, developed the art of keeping ourselves dry, and we make the best rainwear in the world.

Speaking of amber fluids, as we were, if one has overindulged in the national drink, we have another, renowned for its curative qualities and now exported in huge bulk to thirst-stricken hangover sufferers the world over. I speak of course of the golden potion invented by Mr Barr, a can of which I once purchased in Moscow, unable to believe my luck.

Another thing that God and/or complex chemical processes makes in huge quantities in Scotland is scenery, and more and more people are coming to see it. VisitScotland reports that visitor figures are increasing year on year, and they are not taking any of the scenery away with them. What they are taking away is the above-mentioned tartan, shortbread, *uisge* and all the rest, plus, one hopes, happy memories of warmth and hospitality.

Inhabiting this scenery, apart from a race of brilliant inventors respected everywhere, is some of the tastiest food to be had on the planet. Wild salmon, game of all kinds, like a venison stew that an old shepherd of my acquaintance, Archie by name, used to make in vast quantities, and that melted in your mouth, leaving behind a distillation of flavours from heaven. And what do the Beefeaters in the Tower of London prefer when they are chomping their beef? Aberdeen Angus, that's what, and Beefeaters with a capital B should know what's best.

Our lobsters, crabs, prawns et cetera are shipped to the best restaurants everywhere and Loch Fyne has got so many delicious oysters that they are selling them. A dozen of those plump beauties, a daud of lemon, some crusty brown bread, fresh butter and a crisp white wine. Who are you going to change places with?

Cloned sheep, anyone? New inventions emerge from Scotland's scientists and engineers with an amazing rapidity, like the MRI scanner or the Tuley tube (the plastic tree shelter that can be spotted along hillsides and motorway verges around the world). Others, like the groundbreaking animal cloning at the Roslin Institute outside Edinburgh, have spread the fact of Scotland as a place at the cutting edge of technology. A world without cancer? We're working on it. Intelligent machines? Oh aye, and other minor things, like developing wind, air and sea power that will do said minor things, like change the face of the world. Forever.

Ditto. And the rest.

We are often quite backward at putting ourselves forward, but we are no bad at the odd thing or two, when left alone to get on with it.

And we can prove it.

3

Discusses One Clueless Eejit for Longer than He Deserves

David Bowie, who lives in New York, was good enough to ask us, through an interpreter, Kate Moss, who had obviously picked up on Scottish nuances, to: 'Stay with *us*.' I've always fancied New York, so I've booked with David for the first fortnight in August. My mate Tom has the Glasgow Fair.

This is from weegingerdug, a terrific site, used with permission.

Wowie Bowie
(With absolutely no apologies to David Bowie)

There's god-awful cuts in welfare
And Scotland's saying nae mair
But the Tories are yelling 'no'
Though we've told them we want them to go
And Johann is nowhere to be seen
As she walks through the shattered dream
Of a party that's gone true blue
Labour's hooked to the Tory scheme

But Westminster's a saddening bore
For we've seen it ten times or more
So we'll spit in the eyes of fools
As Scotland will focus on
MPs lying through their back teeth
Oh man!
Look at those cavemen go
It's the Commons freak show
Take a look at the pressman
Feeding all the Scots lies,
Oh man! But we already know
It's a one-sided show
There's no truth with Marr.
It's to Osborne's threatening vow
That our country will not kowtow
And we Scots will rule our ain hame
So we can't be sold out again
By the media's ignorant hordes
And careerists and the hopes they've whored
So we'll keep on using the pound
And are deaf to the scares of clowns
Cause Westminster's a saddening bore
And we've stood it ten times or more
Vote no and it comes again
And that's why we focus on
Food banks stretching down the high street
Oh man!

But what would a rich singer know
About this Tory freak show
Take a look at the pressman
Feeding all the Scots lies,
Oh man! But we already know
It's just the Westminster show
There's no truth with Marr.

A Heartfelt Letter to David Bowie: We Could Be Heroes, *Für Einen Tag*

Dear David,

We've been friends a long time. *I keep forgettin'* to contact you, but I was prompted by your comments at the Brits to do so. You've been through a lot of *changes* over the years, and I understand you want Scotland to *stay* in the United Kingdom. I would really like to change your mind.

I know what you're thinking: '*What in the world* is wrong with you?' Surely I'm *a lad insane*. I must be *dancing out in space*. But *can you hear me* out on this one, please?

Here's the thing. *I wish you would* reconsider. You clearly have a *sense of doubt* about this. But I want you to *join the gang* of folk supporting independence. A lot of people in Scotland are *under pressure* economically due to the policies of the ConDem coalition. You know, *it ain't easy* when you're stuck with the bedroom tax, or on what amount to poverty wages, as *some are*.

What's the *fascination* with independence? Well, we don't think it's unfair to ask '*where have all the good times gone?*' And *after all*, it's not as if this is a new thing. It feels like we're always getting lumbered with right-wing governments no matter how we vote – *always crashing in the same car*. So *what in the world* are we to do about it?

The simple fact is that the *shape of things* is different here. We are lucky to have a choice. We don't need to be *sons of the silent age* any more. We don't want to abandon you, and *the next day* after independence will be much like the prior one.

But *I can't explain* how much difference the potential of independence could make over *time*. It's all about *growing up* – a belief that our *golden years* are ahead of us. And we could *move on* from the state of affairs where our legislature is comprised of *scary monsters* like George Osborne and *kooks* like Priti Patel. *Jump, they say*, and Scotland has to say 'how high'. In fact, we'd *rather be high* than have to put up with these idiots any longer.

And the No campaign is a joke. We're expected to listen to the angry ramblings of Alistair Darling, *the man who sold the world,* for goodness' sake. *God only knows* how many more scare stories we'll have to put up with before the vote, but we're confident that we're *right* about this. And we feel confident that we're going to *win*.

Think of it like this. When you moved to Berlin to hang out with Iggy, it was very much *a new career in a new town*. You wanted a new start. And you became even more creative. We're looking for the same chance. And we aren't going to get it in the UK, *anyway, anyhow, anywhere*.

We aren't *absolute beginners* at this stuff: Scotland is a wealthy country which governs itself in health and education: why not everything else? *It's no game*, nor just a *conversation piece*. It offers a reasonable opportunity to *shake it* up and make this country a fairer place, and forget about *all the madmen* in Westminster.

Our reasoning is *sound. And vision* – what vision we have! From the common weal to National Collective, we're not short of *heroes*. In *time*, I think you'll look back on this and forget your panic, realising that *everything's alright* in Scotland, and that we have a healthier relationship for it.

It's not about *loving the alien* – that's not how we think of you. Rather, it's a new form of *modern love* between equal partner nations. From *Neukölln* to *Warszawa*, we'll be welcomed as new members of the international community, and we would love you to be part of that.

We just hope you won't *look back in anger* if we make this choice. It might take us *five years* or more to see the benefits, but it'll be a *fantastic voyage* regardless.

4

Schadenfreude, Angst and the No-voters

How do you get ten No-voters into a Mini?

Say one of them is at Westminster and the others will crawl up his arse.

Sanjeev Kohli, who as well as being a no bad actor at all and having a First in maths from Glasgow Uni, is a twittermeister *sans pareil*. He recently pointed out to his followers, 'There's a spare unit between our local fishmongers and ironmongers. Perhaps Better Together would like to open a scaremongers there.'

Any crisis, large or small, can be dealt with by Bitter Together by following their standard four-stage plan. The instructions for this are as follows:

1. 'We don't think there is a problem. No action needs to be taken. Try and scare the shit out of them anyway.'

2. 'There may be a slight problem, but it's not our place to try to do anything about it. Try and scare the shit out of them anyway.'

3. 'There may well be a problem, but we must consider all possible courses of action and not rush into anything. Try and scare the shit out of them anyway.'
4. 'Well, perhaps we could have done something, but it's too late now. Try and scare the shit out of them anyway.'

Bitter Together have recently changed their emblem from that stupid wee curved triangular thing to a condom, as it more accurately reflects their political stance. A condom needs inflation, halts production, destroys the next generation, protects a bunch of pricks, and gives you a sense of security while you are actually being fucked.

How can you tell an Englishman is sexually excited?
By the stiff upper lip.

The major difference between the English and the Scottish is that the English have good neighbours.

A woman was in bed with her lover and had just told him how stupid her No-voting man was when the door was thrown open and there stood her husband. He glared at her lover and bellowed, 'Whit are you daen?'
'There,' said the wife, 'did ah no say he was stupid?'

Advice to Yes-voters on the unlikely appearance of a No-canvasser at your door:

Do not drive them away with scorn and derision. They are extremely rare beasties and appreciate a little human warmth. They don't get a lot of it and they certainly don't bring any.

Invite them in. Offer them a glass of wine or a wee cup of tea or a coffee. Maybe with a bit of shortie or a digestive.

Have a chat. Listen to their ideas without snorting. Take up as much of their time as you can stand. It's for the cause, because every minute that you keep them talking means that they are not bothering some other poor soul.

As you usher them politely out, don't forget to mention that your entire block, close or street is on holiday.

Incidentally, has anyone ever seen anyone wearing a 'No' badge?

Frankie Boyle has a line that goes, 'In Scotland we have mixed feelings about global warming, because we will get to sit on the mountains and watch the English drown.'

Don't quite get the 'mixed feelings' bit, Frankie.

A No-voter is a man who feels badly when he feels good for fear he'll feel worse when he feels better.

5
Chancellors and Chancers

All things bright and beautiful, all creatures great and small, all things wise and wonderful, Gideon Osborne hates them all.

And it is mutual.

Gideon Osborne is to conciliation what King Herod was to babysitting.

All of the new Scottish currency will be in simplified form, with a large and small unit. This will make it easier for George (né Gideon) Osborne, a chancellor who 'doesn't get' economics, to understand. Yes, punsters, we all wish there was nae Gideon, which, incidentally, means 'The Destroyer' in the original Hebrew.

There will be:

The dreichma, and the dreichda, which, as well as being currency units, are handy answers to your parents' queries about the weather.

The punt and the yankee. As we are taking a wee gamble on ourselves, the revival of the old Irish currency seems appropriate. My chum Tom points out that there might be a problem, because most of the punts at time of writing are in Somerset saving people from the floods.

There is also some difficulty with the yankee, as they seem to be distributed around the world, most of them heavily armed.

The up and the under. Related to the above punt, these terms will be used to describe the relative positions of the Scottish and English currencies in a couple of years' time in the world markets.

The gingy and the jamjaur: local currencies in Glasgow.

The muckle and the meikle: in which we perceive a situation where a mannie with many meikles, weighed down heavily by what we used to call shrapnel, smash or small change, goes into a bank, almost certainly not the Royal Bank of Scotland, and asks: 'Ahv ower mony meikles. Ony chance ye could mak these meikles mak a muckle?'

6

Scaremongering? I'll Give You Scaremongering

Professor Steve Bruce, of the School of Social Science at Aberdeen University, knows that the Scots just looove lies and condescension. In fact, the only thing we love more than these is irony. He penned the following:

The Yes camp is wrong to accuse No campaigners of scare tactics. The future will be far worse than anything we have been told thus far.

If Scotland becomes independent, it will lose access to GPS, the internet and all telephony. Music will be reduced to the Alexander Brothers, television to *White Heather Club* reruns. It will rain all the time, except when it is snowing. No foreigners (and that includes the English) will enter the country.

All Scottish businesses will relocate to Swindon. All the fish in Scottish waters will immediately swim to countries in the EU (which will include every Eastern European economic basket case, but not Scotland). A plague of locusts will destroy all crops except oats, and cuisine will be reduced to porridge. The sun will not rise above Berwick. Do not say you were not warned.

7
High (and Low) Jinks and Haughmagandie

A ravingly negative and endlessly boring No-voter on holiday in Troon was asking about sexual possibilities in the town and was told that the church had driven all the loose women out of the town but that they still operated in caves up in the hills at the back.

'It's very simple,' said his Yes-voting local informant. 'You go up there and shout "Yoo-hoo-hoo!" outside the cave. If there is no answer, then she is busy but, if she shouts, "Yoo-hoo-hoo!" back, you go in and negotiate.'

That evening the No-voter climbed up to the cave and shouted, but there was no reply so he decided to go back to the pub. On the way back, he came across another big cave at the foot of the hill, so he went to the entrance and shouted, 'Yoo-hoo-hoo!' as loud as he could.

'Yoo-hoo, yoo-hoo-oo-oo-oo!' replied the cave. Full of excitement, the No-voter rushed into the dark entrance and was run over by the 8.30 from Glasgow.

One of those enormous braying English women, one of the ones wearing two-inch-thick tweed who is always married to some Scottish lord and who is always at the next table to you in a restaurant, talking louder than you can shout, goes into the Rangers shop at Ibrox with her two boys, both of them wearing England tops.

'BRAND-NEW ENGLAND TOPS FOR MY SONS,' she commands.

The guy behind the counter asks, 'Are they twins?'

'NO,' replies the woman. 'NIGEL IS SEVEN AND PEREGRINE IS EIGHT.'

'Really?' says the sales assistant.

'WHY SO INCREDULOUS?' she says. 'DO THEY LOOK IDENTICAL TO YOU?'

'Naw,' says the guy behind the counter. 'I just can't believe somebody's shagged you twice.'

What do you call a Scotsman flying a plane?

The pilot, you English bastard.

They say the Commonwealth Games is going to rekindle Scottish national pride. Jesus, for a budget of £1.2 billion you could've written 'Vote Yes, Please' in very large letters on the moon.

There's a wee Glasgow laddie down in Blackpool with his dad and he asks to go to the Pleasure Beach. He has been on everything from the dodgems to the helter-skelter to the ghost train. His dad leaves him for a minute to go to the loo, telling him not to move an inch till he gets back.

The wee boy sees a balloon floating past and runs after it, as they do. Then he realises that he's lost in the crowd and starts howling.

A policewoman, one of Lancashire's finest, sees him and comes over and asks what's up.

He sobs, 'Ah've loast ma faither an' he'll kill me cos ah wisnae tae move until he goat back fae huvvin' a pish but ah saw a balloon an' chased it and ah goat loast an' he'll kill me!' Sniff.

The policewoman says, 'Calm down, lad. We'll find him. Now, what's your dad like?'

The boy looks at her hopefully and says, 'Rangers, wummin wi' big tits, an' goin' tae the pub fur a bevvy.'

An Englishman lecturing on his travels was speaking disparagingly about the Scots in Canada and the mixing of the race with the indigenous folk.

'You'll find,' he said, 'a great number of Scots half-breeds and French half-breeds, but you cannot find any English half-breeds.'

'Not surprising,' shouted a Scot in the audience. 'The women had to draw the line somewhere.'

'My father was SNP and his father before him was SNP,' said the young man who had just received his vote and was engaged in the age-old argument on politics. With a flourish, he added, 'And I'm going to be SNP too.'

His friend asked, 'Suppose your father was a fool and his father before him was a fool, what, according to your argument, should you be?'

The friend was not prepared for the quick answer: 'An English MP.'

'How long will it take me to walk into the village from here?' enquired the English tourist.

'No idea,' replied the farmer.

Off trudged the Englishman, muttering to himself.

'Come back,' called the farmer.

'What now?' asked the tourist.

'It'll take you about ten minutes.'

'Why didn't you tell me that in the first place?' asked the Englishman.

'I didn't know how fast you walked.'

Another Scottish farmer, despite the Westminster red-tape machinations, set up his own small industry manufacturing mechanical turnip snaggers. At present, up to fifteen snaggers an hour are rolling off the assembly line. Production will be higher when the snaggers stop rolling off the assembly line.

Two No-voters were discussing the beauties of nature and the coming of spring.

'I see that the snowdrops are out early this year,' said one.

'How will that affect us?' asked the other.

'Oh, badly, badly, I've no doubt.'

A Scottish farmer was in his field digging up his tatties. An English farmer looked over the fence and said, 'In Devon we grow potatoes five times larger than that.'

The Scotsman replied, 'Grow them to fit your mouths, dae ye?'

The fantasy of every Scots woman is to have two male No-voters. One cleaning and the other dusting.

On a tour of Scotland, the Pope took a couple of days off his itinerary to visit the north coast near Aberdeen on an impromptu sightseeing trip. His 4x4 Popemobile was driving along the golden sands when there was an enormous commotion heard just off the headland. They rushed to see what it was and, upon approaching the scene, the Pope noticed, in the surf, a hapless man wearing an England top struggling frantically to free himself from the jaws of a twenty-foot-long shark.

At that moment, a speedboat containing three men wearing Scottish football tops roared into view from around the point. Spontaneously, one of the men took aim and fired a harpoon into the shark's ribs, immobilising it instantly. The other two reached out and pulled the man from the water and then, using long clubs, beat the shark to death.

They bundled the bleeding, semi-conscious man into the speedboat along with the dead shark and then prepared for a hasty retreat, when they heard frantic shouting from the shore. It was, of course, the Pope, and he summoned them to the beach.

Upon them reaching the shore, the Pope went into raptures about the rescue and said, 'I give you my blessing for your brave actions. I had heard that there were some racist, xenophobic people trying to divide Scotland and England but now I have seen with my own eyes this is not true. I can see that your society is a truly enlightened example of racial harmony and could serve as a model which other nations could follow.' He blessed them all and drove off in a flurry of sand.

As he departed, the harpoonist asked the others, 'Who was that?'

'That,' one answered, 'was his Holiness the Pope.

He is in direct contact with God and has access to all God's wisdom. He is supposed to be infallible.'

'Well,' the harpoonist replied, 'he can't be all that infallible cos he knows fuck all about shark fishing. Is that bait holding up, or do we need to get another one? There's a No-voter in the boot of the car.'

One Saturday, a family of Westminster types head out Christmas shopping. While in JJB Sports, the son picks up a Scotland shirt and says to his sister, 'I've decided I'm going to be a Scotland supporter and I would like this shirt for my Christmas.'

The sister is outraged at this, promptly whacks him round the head and says, 'Go and talk to our mother.'

Off goes the little lad, with Scotland shirt in hand, and finds his mother. 'Mum?'

'Yes, son?'

'I've decided I'm going to be a Scotland supporter and I would like this shirt for my Christmas.'

The mother is outraged at this, promptly whacks him round the head and says, 'Go and talk to your father.'

Off he goes with the Scotland shirt in hand and finds his father. 'Dad?'

'Yes, son?'

'I've decided I'm going to be a Scotland supporter and I would like this shirt for Christmas.'

The father is outraged at this, promptly whacks his son round the head and says, 'No son of mine is ever going to be seen in THAT!'

About half an hour later, they are all back in the car, heading home. The father turns to the son and says, 'Son, I hope you have learned something today.'

The son turns to his father and says, 'Yes, Father, I have.'

Father says, 'That's good, son. What is it?'

The son replies, 'I've only been a Scotland supporter for an hour and I hate you English bastards already.'

Sandy met Donald, an old friend, after the passage of some years, and the following conversation took place.

'I've been married since I last saw you, Donald.'

'Married, Sandy? That's good.'

'Oh, not so good, Donald – she was a probable No-voter and a terrible scold.'

'Married to a No-voter and a scold, you say? That's very bad, Sandy.'

'Och, not so bad, Donald – she had tons of money.'

'A wife with money, Sandy? That's very, very good.'

'Oh, not so good, Donald – she was very mean-spirited with it. Tight, but not in a good way.'

'A No-voting wife with money, Sandy, and very thrifty with it? That's not good.'

'Och, not so bad, Donald – she built a house with it.'

'A house of your own, Sandy? That's very fine.'

'Not so fine, Donald – the house burned down.'

'The new house built with your wife's money burned down, Sandy? That's very bad indeed.'

'Och, not too bad, Donald. It was insured – and she was in it.'

A rather supercilious No-voting Edinbugger enters a barber's shop in Glasgow for a shave. While the barber is foaming him up, he mentions the problem he has getting a close shave around his sallow and sunken cheeks, 'Especially from you Yes-voting Weegies. You can't seem to do it – like your voting – no attention to detail.'

'Och, I have just the thing,' says the barber, taking a small wooden ball from a nearby drawer. 'Just place this between your cheek and gum.'

The client places the ball in his mouth and the barber proceeds with the closest shave the man has ever experienced.

After a few strokes, the client asks in garbled speech, 'And what if I swallow it?'

'No problem,' says the barber, 'just bring it back tomorrow like everyone else.'

8
Rogues, Vagabonds, Traitors and Right Bastards

99.99% of Scots and English are decent, hard-working, law-abiding and honest citizens. But we still have to learn to accept the blame for electing the other 0.01%.

'But after all, if this prince [Robert the Bruce] shall leave these principles he hath so nobly pursued, and consent that we or our kingdom be subjected to the king or people of England, we will immediately endeavour to expel him, as our enemy and as the subverter both of his own and our rights, and we will make another king, who will defend our liberties; for, so long as there shall but one hundred of us remain alive we will never give consent to subject ourselves to the dominion of the English. For it is not glory, it is not riches, neither is it honour, but it is freedom alone that we fight and contend for, which no honest man will lose but with his life.'

From the Declaration of Arbroath, 1320

Summary:

We, the people of Scotland, are sovereign. We will

elect our own king and elbow him if he is not up to snuff.

And what do we want?

Freedom!

When do we want it?

Now!

'It may be doubted whether the descendants of the noble lords and honourable gentlemen who accepted this gratification would be more shocked at the general fact of their ancestors being corrupted or scandalised at the paltry amount of the bribe.

'One noble lord accepted so low a sum as eleven guineas; and the bargain was the more hard, as he threw his religion into the bargain, and from Catholic turned Protestant, to make the vote a good one.'

Sir Walter Scott on the Treaty of Union

The reasons for the Union of the Parliaments (which was hugely unpopular with the ordinary Scottish people, most of who at that time did not have the vote) were complex and varied.

Many petitions were sent to the Scottish Parliament against the Union, and there were massive protests in Edinburgh and several other Scottish towns on the day it was passed, as threats of widespread civil unrest resulted in the imposition of martial law by the

Parliament. Sir George Lockhart of Carnwath, a Jacobite and the only member of the Scottish negotiating team who was not pro-incorporation, noted that 'the whole nation appears against the Union'.

Sir John Clerk of Penicuik, an ardent pro-unionist and Union negotiator, observed that the treaty was 'contrary to the inclinations of at least three-fourths of the Kingdom'. Public opinion against the treaty as it passed through the Scottish Parliament was voiced through petitions from Scottish localities. Anti-union petitions were received from shires, burghs, presbyteries and parishes. The Convention of Royal Burghs also petitioned against the Union and not one petition in favour of an incorporating union was received by Parliament. On the day the treaty was signed, the carillonneur in St Giles' Cathedral, Edinburgh, rang the bells to the tune 'Why Should I Be So Sad on My Wedding Day?'

From the Union of the Crowns in 1603, England and Scotland had one monarch but two parliaments. While this worked most of the time, there were occasions when the two institutions parted company – such as when England executed King Charles I (to the distress of many in Scotland) and became a republic, while at the same time Scotland's governing body resolved to appoint King Charles II as their monarch. From the perspective of the leaders in

London, such a situation had to be avoided in the future and the removal of the Scottish Parliament was seen as a way of achieving this.

Following the abdication of King James VII and the accession of William and Mary, the Scottish Parliament were in agreement and declared a few months later that James VII had forfeited the Scottish throne. But there were many in Scotland who still supported the deposed monarch. There were even uprisings in Scotland in support of James, and the Jacobite cause was still bubbling away at the turn of the century.

There was still a large measure of religious intolerance in both England and Scotland and those in power were determined that there should never again be a Catholic monarch. But the deposed Stuart line (with their Catholic sympathies) really had a stronger claim on the throne and again there were more in Scotland who felt that this should count. When the English Parliament decided, without consultation with their Scottish counterparts, that the crown should go via the Electress of Hanover, the German granddaughter of King James VI and through her to her son (the future King George I), the Scots Parliament made plain its resentment.

There were a number of poor harvests in Scotland in the 1690s and Scotland's economic position was then drastically worsened by the ill-fated Darien Scheme to create a Scottish colony in Panama. Scotland lost 25% of its liquid assets. The Act of Union undertook to pay £400,000 in compensation to those who had incurred these losses. This was of course blatant bribery, as the people who were to benefit from this compensation were amongst those who had voted in favour of the Union. Some of this was used to hire spies, such as Daniel Defoe. His first reports were of vivid descriptions of violent demonstrations against the Union. 'A Scots rabble is the worst of its kind,' he reported. 'For every Scot in favour there is 99 against.' Years later, John Clerk of Penicuik, a leading Unionist, wrote in his memoirs that 'Defoe was a spy among us, but not known as such, otherwise the Mob of Edinburgh would pull him to pieces'.

Scotland relied on 50% of its exports going to England. In an act of blackmail in 1705, the English Parliament closed its market to Scottish cattle, coal and linen and declared that all Scots would be treated as aliens. It showed the vulnerability of Scotland to a trade war. In addition, Scotland was excluded from England's colonial territories – indeed, early moves towards a union of the parliaments stumbled in England, as they were reluctant to allow open access. But the Act of Union in 1707 created the greatest free trade area in the world at that time.

A commission representing the two bodies met and thrashed out the details. The Scots lost the argument for a federal arrangement but did manage to secure the continuation of the Scottish legal system, education and church. These were important elements in allowing the country to continue to regard itself as a separate entity. The privileges of the Scottish royal burghs were also to be maintained. Debates in the Scottish Parliament were heated and lengthy, while the crowds in the streets burned copies of the treaty and threw stones at the parliament windows. A mob held the city of Glasgow for a month. But, on 16 January 1707, the Treaty of Union was passed by 110 votes to 67 (with more than a suspicion that many Members of Parliament had been bribed, though this was nothing new for those days). The treaty was passed in Westminster without opposition and the Scottish Parliament met for the last time on 25 March 1707.

When the Act of Union was given the Royal Assent by the Earl of Seafield, he touched the document with the royal sceptre, saying, 'There's the end of an auld sang.'

Nearly 300 years later, at the 'reconvening' of Parliament in Edinburgh in 1999, our Presiding Officer Winnie Ewing was to say that it was the 'start of a new sang. The Scottish Parliament, adjourned on the twenty-fifth day of March in the year 1707, is hereby reconvened.'

I know that I wasn't the only one crying.

Such a Parcel o' Rogues in a Nation

Fareweil tae aa' our Scottish fame
Fareweil our ancient glory
Fareweil e'en tae our Scottish name
Sae famed in martial story
Nou Sark rins ower the Solway sands
An' Tweed rins tae the ocean
Tae mark whaur England's province stauns
Sic a parcel o' rogues in a nation!

What force or guile could not subdue
Thro many warlike ages
Is wrocht nou by a coward few
For hireling traitor's wages
The English steel we could disdain
Secure in valour's station
But English gold has been our bane
Sic a parcel o' rogues in a nation!

O wad ere I had seen the day
That treason thus could sell us
My auld gray heid had lain in clay

Wi' Bruce an' loyal Wallace
But pith an' poo'er till my last hour
I'll mak this declaration:
We're bocht an' sold for English gold
Sic a parcel o' rogues in a nation!

Robert Burns
(as sung by Dick Gaughan)

Sir Walter Scott summed up the attitude of the Scottish 'woman in the street' at the time in the words of one of his characters, Mrs Howden, in *Heart of Midlothian*: 'I ken, when we had a king, and a chancellor, and parliament – men o' our ain, we could aye peeble them wi' stones when they werena gude bairns – but naebody's nails can reach the length o' Lunnon.'

And another contemporary versifier had thoughts on the subject:

Verses on the Scots Peers (1706)

Our Duiks were deills, our Marquesses were mad
Our Earls were evil, our Viscounts yet more bad
Our Lords were villains, and our Barons knaves
Who wish our burrows did sell us for slaves.
They sold the church, they sold the State and Nation

Rogues, Vagabonds, Traitors and Right Bastards

They sold their honour, name and reputation
They sold their birthright, peerages and places
And now they leave the House with angrie faces.

9
The Mither Tung

We might have the odd thing or two to thank England for, but their spelling and pronunciation are not included. Let's face it – English is a seriously daft language.

There's no ham in a hamburger, and neither apple nor pine in pineapple. Sweetmeats are sweet, while sweetbreads, which aren't sweet, are meat. We take English for granted, but if we explore its paradoxes, we find that quicksand can work slowly, boxing rings are square and a guinea pig is neither from Guinea and nor is it a pig.

And why is it that writers write but fingers don't fing, grocers don't groce and hammers don't ham? If the plural of tooth is teeth, why isn't the plural of booth beeth? One goose, two geese; one moose, two meese; one index, two indices? Doesn't it seem a bit silly that you can make amends but not one amend, that you comb through the annals of history but not a single annal?

If you have a bunch of odds and ends and get rid of all but one of them, what do you call it? If teachers taught, why didn't preachers praught? If a vegetarian eats vegetables, what does a humanitarian eat?

Sometimes I think all the English speakers should be committed to an asylum for the verbally insane. In what language do people recite at a play and play at a recital? Ship by lorry and send cargo by ship? Have noses that run and feet that smell?

How can a slim chance and a fat chance be the same, while a wise man and a wise guy are opposites? How can overlook and oversee be opposites, while quite a lot and quite a few are alike? How can the weather be hot as hell one day and cold as hell another? Have you noticed that we talk about certain things only when they are absent? Have you ever seen a horseful carriage or a strapful dress? Met a sung hero or experienced requited love? Have you ever run into someone who was combobulated, gruntled, ruly or peccable? And where are all those people who ARE spring chickens or who would ACTUALLY hurt a fly?

You have to marvel at the unique lunacy of a language in which your house can burn up as it burns down, in which you fill in a form by filling it out and in which an alarm clock goes off by going on.

English was invented by people, not computers, and it reflects the creativity of the human race (which, of course, isn't a race at all). That is why when the stars are out they are visible, but when the lights are out they are invisible. And why, when I wind up my watch, I start it, but when I wind up this nonsense, I end it.

Scotland vs England

The first known version of 'The Chaos' appeared as an appendix to the fourth edition of Dutchman Dr Gerard Nolst Trenité's schoolbook *Drop Your Foreign Accent* or, as he put it, *engelsche uitspraakoefeningen*. We talk of little else over breakfast in Glasgow's West End.

A Wee Poem in English (aka The Chaos)

Dearest creature in creation,
Study English pronunciation.
I will teach you in my verse
Sounds like corpse, corps, horse, and worse.
I will keep you, Suzy, busy,
Make your head with heat grow dizzy.
Tear in eye, your dress will tear.
So shall I! Oh hear my prayer.
Pray, console your loving poet,
Make my coat look new, dear, sew it!

Just compare heart, beard, and heard,
Dies and diet, lord and word,
Sword and sward, retain and Britain.
(Mind the latter, how it's written.)
Now I surely will not plague you
With such words as plaque and ague.
But be careful how you speak:

The Mither Tung

Say break and steak, but bleak and streak;
Cloven, oven, how and low,
Script, receipt, show, poem, and toe.

Hear me say, devoid of trickery,
Daughter, laughter, and Terpsichore,
Typhoid, measles, topsails, aisles,
Exiles, similes, and reviles;
Scholar, vicar, and cigar,
Solar, mica, war and far;
One, anemone, Balmoral,
Kitchen, lichen, laundry, laurel;
Gertrude, German, wind and mind,
Scene, Melpomene, mankind.

Billet does not rhyme with ballet,
Bouquet, wallet, mallet, chalet.
Blood and flood are not like food,
Nor is mould like should and would.
Viscous, viscount, load and broad,
Toward, to forward, to reward.
And your pronunciation's OK
When you correctly say croquet,
Rounded, wounded, grieve and sieve,
Friend and fiend, alive and live.

Scotland vs England

Ivy, privy, famous; clamour
And enamour rhyme with hammer.
River, rival, tomb, bomb, comb,
Doll and roll and some and home.
Stranger does not rhyme with anger,
Neither does devour with clangour.
Souls but foul, haunt but aunt,
Font, front, wont, want, grand, and grant,
Shoes, goes, does. Now first say finger,
And then singer, ginger, linger,
Real, zeal, mauve, gauze, gouge and gauge,
Marriage, foliage, mirage, and age.

Query does not rhyme with very,
Nor does fury sound like bury.
Dost, lost, post and doth, cloth, loth.
Job, nob, bosom, transom, oath.
Though the differences seem little,
We say actual but victual.
Refer does not rhyme with deafer.
Foeffer does, and zephyr, heifer.
Mint, pint, senate and sedate;
Dull, bull, and George ate late.
Scenic, Arabic, Pacific,
Science, conscience, scientific.

The Mither Tung

Liberty, library, heave and heaven,
Rachel, ache, moustache, eleven.
We say hallowed, but allowed,
People, leopard, towed, but vowed.
Mark the differences, moreover,
Between mover, cover, clover;
Leeches, breeches, wise, precise,
Chalice, but police and lice;
Camel, constable, unstable,
Principle, disciple, label.

Petal, panel, and canal,
Wait, surprise, plait, promise, pal.
Worm and storm, chaise, chaos, chair,
Senator, spectator, mayor.
Tour, but our and succour, four.
Gas, alas, and Arkansas.
Sea, idea, Korea, area,
Psalm, Maria, but malaria.
Youth, south, southern, cleanse and clean.
Doctrine, turpentine, marine.
Compare alien with Italian,
Dandelion and battalion.
Sally with ally, yea, ye,
Eye, I, ay, aye, whey, and key.
Say aver, but ever, fever,
Neither, leisure, skein, deceiver.

Scotland vs England

Heron, granary, canary.
Crevice and device and aerie.

Face, but preface, not efface.
Phlegm, phlegmatic, ass, glass, bass.
Large, but target, gin, give, verging,
Ought, out, joust and scour, scourging.
Ear, but earn and wear and tear
Do not rhyme with here but ere.
Seven is right, but so is even,
Hyphen, roughen, nephew Stephen,
Monkey, donkey, Turk and jerk,
Ask, grasp, wasp, and cork and work.

Pronunciation – think of Psyche!
Is a paling stout and spikey?
Won't it make you lose your wits,
Writing teats and saying tits?
It's a dark abyss or tunnel,
Strewn with stones, stowed, solace, gunwale,
Islington and Isle of Wight,
Housewife, verdict and indict.

Finally, which rhymes with enough –
Though, through, plough, or dough, or cough?
Hiccough has the sound of cup.
My advice is to give up!

And a wee taste of Scots:

Did you hear about the Highlander who found a trumpet growing in his garden?

He rootit it oot.

10
Magic Stanes and the Like

The Wee Magic Stane

The Dean o' Westminster was a powerful man
He held a' the strings o' the State in his hand
But wi' a' his great business it flustered him nane
When some rogues ran away wi' his wee magic stane
Wi' a too-ra-li-oo-ra-li-oo-ra-li-ay

(Alternative chorus, from Archie Fisher, if memory
serves, 'Singin', "Ah'm a ban-the-bomber, who's a ban-
the-bomber? Ah'm a ban-the-bomber, me"')

The Stane had great powers that could dae sic a thing
That withoot it it seemed we'd be wantin' a king
So he sent for the polis and made this decree
Go hunt oot the Stone and return it tae me
Wi' a too-ra-li-oo-ra-li-oo-ra-li-ay

So the polis went beetlin' up tae the north
They hunted the Clyde and they hunted the Forth
But the wild folk up yonder just kidded them a'
For they didnae believe it was magic at a'
Wi' a too-ra-li-oo-ra-li-oo-ra-li-ay

Magic Stanes and the Like

Noo the Provost o' Glesca, Sir Victor by name
Wis awfy pit oot when he heard o' the Stane
So he offered the statues that stan' in George Square
That the High Church's masons might mak' a few
mair
Wi' a too-ra-li-oo-ra-li-oo-ra-li-ay

When the Dean o' Westminster wi' this was acquaint
He sent for Sir Victor and made him a saint
'But it's no good you sending your statues down heah'
Said the Dean, 'But it gives me a jolly good ideah'
Wi' a too-ra-li-oo-ra-li-oo-ra-li-ay

So they quarried a stane o' the very same stuff
And they dressed it all up till it looked like enough
Then he sent for the press and announced that the
Stane
Had been found and returned tae Westminster again
Wi' a too-ra-li-oo-ra-li-oo-ra-li-ay

When the reivers found oot what Westminster had
done
They went aboot diggin' up stanes by the ton
And fur each wan they feenished they entered the
claim
That THIS was the true and original stane
Wi' a too-ra-li-oo-ra-li-oo-ra-li-ay

But the cream o' the jest still remains tae be telt
For the bloke that wis turnin' them aff on the belt
At the peak o' production was sae sorely pressed
That the real yin got bunged in alang wi' the rest
Wi' a too-ra-li-oo-ra-li-oo-ra-li-ay

So if ever ye come on a stane wi' a ring
Just sit yersel' doon and proclaim yersel' king
There's nane will be able tae challenge yer claim
That ye've crooned yersel' King on the Destiny Stane
Wi' a too-ra-li-oo-ra-li-oo-ra-li-ay

Trad./Johnny McAvoy
(As sung by Robin Hall and Jimmie MacGregor)

The Stone of Scone, on which the Bruce was crowned, is a basic symbol of Scottish culture and nationalism. Therefore, it was 'rehoused' in Westminster Abbey by the English. It disappeared on Christmas Day 1951. There was considerable investigation and a similar stone was eventually recovered. Several forged copies were then displayed which were identical to the 'recovered' one. The Scots thought this was pretty funny and enough songs appeared to honour the circumstances to be published in a small book, *Sangs o' the Stane*.

The whereabouts of the original is still an open question, though I'm sure that I've sat on it. They had it at the People's Palace in Glasgow a few years back and I stepped over the rope, sat down and proclaimed myself king. I've never used my power, as I am a republican.

This reacquirement (never call it a theft – it's ours) captured the imagination – and the sense of humour – of all of Scotland. For example, the story went that one suspect was hauled in for questioning. After hours of fierce examination under a bright light, he at last said wearily, 'All right, all right. Turn that thing off and I'll tell you who stole it.'

They leaned forward eagerly. 'Right, who stole it?'

'Edward the First,' he replied.

And now it is back. And it is still ours. Who is up for defending it? Aye, me too.

11
Loyalty and Royalty

Loyalty is all. Clan, country and friends, in that order. There are many recorded examples of this very distinctive Scottish trait.

'After all,' said the old widow, while being consoled on the loss of her husband, 'he wasn't a drop of blood kin to me.'

This reply recalls the real-life domestic problem of a Scot whose sister had been living with his wife and himself for many years. But two women is one too many in any house and finally the situation could be endured no longer. One of the women had to leave. Blood is blood. He asked his wife to leave.

When Jock moved to London, he constantly annoyed his English friends by boasting about how great Scotland was. Finally, in exasperation, one said, 'If Scotland's so marvellous, why is it that you didn't stay there?'

'Well,' explained Jock, 'they're all so clever in

Scotland I had to cross the Border to have any chance of making it at all.'

An Englishman, roused by a Scot's scorn of his race, protested that he was born an Englishman and hoped to die an Englishman.

'Man,' scoffed the Scot, 'have you no ambition at all?'

A modest Scotsman speaking of his family said, 'The Douglas family is a very, very old Scottish family. The line runs back into antiquity. We don't know how far back it goes, but it's a long, long way back, and the history of the Douglas family is recorded in five volumes. In about the middle of the third volume, a note in the margin reads, "Around this time the world was created."'

'Speaking of old families,' said the snobbish Englishman, 'one of my ancestors was present at the signing of the Magna Carta.'

'And one of mine,' said another Scot, 'was at the signing of the Ten Commandments.'

A clansman who was lame in one leg was laughed at on the night of the battle against England by the rest of the footsoldiers because of his lameness.

'I'm here to stand and fight,' he said, 'not to run.'

A woman was stopped on the street by a down-at-heel Scotsman.

'Could you spare a pound for something to eat, ma'am?'

'Why are you begging, a big strong man like you? I would think you'd be ashamed.'

'Madam,' he said, removing his hat and bowing, 'I am a sad and disappointed Highland romantic. I have woven dreams of cobweb stuff and the wild west wind has swept them away. They lie in the detritus of history. And so I have turned to this profession – the only one I know in which a Scottish gentleman can address the most beautiful woman in all of England without the formality of an introduction.'

Yes, of course he got a tenner.

An Englishman, an Irishman and a Scotsman were asked in a survey what nationality they would like to have been born if they hadn't been born the nationality they were.

'If I hadn't been born English,' said the Englishman, 'I would have liked to have been French.'

'If I hadn't been born Irish,' said the Irishman, 'I would have liked to have been Scottish.'

'If I hadn't been born Scottish,' said the Scotsman, 'I would have been ashamed of myself.'

The Bannockburn guide had shown some English visitors over the battlefield. For his services and his graphic descriptions of the events of that day of days, he had been offered a nice tip. 'No, no, keep your money,' he replied with great self-denial. 'This battlefield has cost you enough already.'

The same guide was describing the various battles won by the Scots over the centuries, when an English visitor protested that the English must have won at least some of the battles. The guide turned on his microphone really loudly and announced: 'Not on this bus.'

A philosophical Scotland supporter on the train south to attend the England–Scotland game was heard to comment, 'No matter if we win or lose this game, we will still be winners in the game of life because, when our opponents waken up tomorrow, they'll still be English and we won't.'

The Pope and Queen Elizabeth I of Scotland were in the stand at the Scotland–England game, beaming at the thousands of people below. The Queen said to the Pope out of the side of her mouth, 'I bet you a tenner that I can make every English person in the crowd go wild with just a wave of my hand.'

The Pope replied, 'No way! You can't do that.'

The Queen said, 'Watch this!' So the Queen waved her hand and every English person in the crowd went crazy, waving their little plastic Union Jacks on sticks and cheering like mad.

The Pope was standing there thinking, 'Oh, no, what am I going to do? I never thought she'd be able to do it.' He thought to himself for a minute and then turned to her and said, 'I bet you I can make every Scottish person in the crowd go wild – not just now, but for the rest of the week – with just one nod of my head.'

The Queen replied, 'No way, it can't be done.'

So the Pope stuck the head on her.

This joke is so old that it has recently received a grant from Historic Scotland – still funny, though.

Edward Longshanks (Edward I of England) travels north to attempt to conquer the Scots and brings 4,000 men with him. As he nears the battlefield, there appears a solitary figure on the crest of the hill. It is a short, ginger-haired man in a kilt.

'Hammer o' the Scots, is it?' he yells. 'Come up here, ya English eejits, and we'll see who does the hammerin'."

Edward turns to his commander. 'Send twenty men to deal with that upstart, there's a good chap,' he says.

The commander sends twenty of his best men over the hill to kill the Scotsman.

Ten minutes later, at the crest of the hill, the little Scot appears again. 'Ya English bampots,' he yells. 'Come on, the rest of ye! Come on, I'll gub the lot o' ye.'

Edward is now very annoyed. He turns to his commander and says, 'Send a hundred men to kill that little guttersnipe!'

The commander sends a hundred men over the hill to do the job.

Ten minutes later, the little Scot appears at the top of the hill once more, his hair all sticking up, his shirt a wee bit torn. 'Ya English SCUM!' he yells. 'I'm just warming up! Come and get me, ya English gets!'

Edward loses patience. 'Commander, take 400 men and WIPE HIM OFF THE EARTH!' he yells.

The commander gulps but leads 400 men on horseback over the crest of the hill.

Ten minutes later, the little Scotsman is back. His clothing is all torn and his face is covered in blood, snotters and Irn-Bru. 'Is that the best ye can do? You're bloody WIMMIN! Come on! Come and have a go, ya bunch of English jessies!' he yells.

Edward turns to his second-in-command. 'Take a thousand men over that hill and don't come back till you've killed him!' he orders.

The second-in-command gathers the men and they ride off over the hill.

Ten minutes later, one of the English troops crawls back over the top of the hill. He's bleeding from every orifice, covered in blood and his clothes are in tatters. 'Your Majesty!' he yells. 'It's a trap! There's TWO of them!'

A No-voter, a Yes-voter, an Irishman and a Welshman were travelling in an aircraft that went out of control and was about to crash. To their dismay, they discovered that there were only three parachutes on the plane.

The No-voter argued that he ought to have one since he was a very important businessman whose death would result in the collapse of the stock market and would force the move of his company to England.

The Yes-voter, shaking his head ruefully, handed him over a pack and the No-voter bailed out.

Next, the Irishman argued that he should be given a parachute. He was an important politician upon whom all hope of peace in Ireland rested. And they already had their independence. He silently put the straps over his shoulders and jumped out after the No-voter.

The Yes-voter now turned to the Welshman and handed him a parachute. 'Here you are, Celtic brother,' he said cheerfully.

'But what about you?' gasped the Welshman, amazed at this unflinching heroism.

'Oh, I'll be all right,' said the Yes-voter. 'I gave the No-voter my haversack.'

How do you know when a No-voter is about to say something intelligent?

When he starts his sentence with, 'A Yes-voter once told me . . .'

A wee Scottish boy, generally known about the English village his parents had moved to as being not too intelligent, was annoying the busy blacksmith. Hoping to scare him away, the blacksmith finally held a red-hot piece of iron under the boy's nose.

'If you give me a pound, I'll lick it,' said the simple-looking youngster.

The blacksmith held out the coin.

Without a word, the boy took the coin, licked it, dropped it into his pocket and, whistling softly, walked away.

Scotsman: 'Why is English beer like having sex in a canoe?'

Englishman: 'Dunno, why?'

Scotsman: 'Because it's fucking close to water!'

It was the England vs Scotland match at Wembley. The MacGregor brothers approached the turnstile.

'How much is it?' asked Calum.

'Twenty pounds,' said the ticket seller.

'Well, I've only got one eye so I'm only paying ten.' And, wonder of wonders, the man let him in.

'And I'm only paying ten pounds,' said Hamish.

'Hang on,' said the turnstile keeper, 'you've got two eyes.'

'Aye,' said Hamish, 'but I've only come to see Scotland.'

Sandy called the stationmaster. 'I left a bottle of malt whisky on the train this morning,' he said. 'Was it turned in to the lost and found department?'

'No,' said the mannie, 'but the Englishman who found it was. Would you like a kick at him?'

A Scottish geologist has established that Scotland is bigger than England because of its mountains. If Scotland were rolled out as flat as England, it would be the bigger country of the two.

'These rock formations,' explained the tourist-worn guide, 'were piled up here in the Highlands by the glaciers.'

'Where are the glaciers now?' asked the female English tourist.

'They've gone back, madam, to get more,' said the guide.

During an excursion to the Isle of Lewis, the weather turned cold and rainy and the passengers huddled together for warmth. The boat captain shouted down to the crew's quarters. 'Is there a mackintosh down there large enough to keep three English ladies warm?'

'No,' came the booming answer, 'but there's a MacPherson who'd like to try.'

12
The Golf

Irate English golfer, on his way to a round of 150: 'You must be the worst caddy in the world!'

Scottish caddy, drily: 'That would be too much of a coincidence, sir.'

English golfer, far off in the rough on the Old Course: 'Hey, caddy, why do you keep looking at your watch?'

Caddie: 'It isn't a watch, sir, it's a compass.'

Jimmy's playing golf with his wife and he's par all the way round for the first time ever, but he shanks his drive behind a big barn on the par four eighteenth and there is no chance of him getting a shot on the green.

'Hold on,' says his wife, a very organised English lady. 'Let's open the front doors of the barn and then the back doors. You could then whack it right through the middle and onto the green. You might even get a birdie.'

So they do that, but he shanks the ball again. It hits off a great big cross-beam, ricochets down onto his wife's head and kills her stone dead.

A year to the day later, he is playing the same course

with his dead wife's brother, a very organised Englishman. Jimmy is once again par when they tee off at the last and he once again shanks the ball into the same spot, right behind the barn.

'Hold on,' says the brother-in-law. 'Let's open the front doors of the barn and then the back doors. You could then whack it right through the middle and onto the green. You might even get a birdie.'

Jimmy falls to his knees, tears in his eyes and says, 'Sorry, Nigel, but I just can't. The last time I did this was when your sister died . . . and I ended up with a nine.'

Earth flew in all directions as the crimson-faced English would-be golfer attempted to strike the ball. 'My word,' he blurted out to his caddy, 'the worms will think there's been an earthquake.'

'I don't know,' replied the caddy. 'The worms are nae sae blate here in St Andrews. I think most of them are hiding underneath the ball for safety.'

Some golfers were watching the final stages of a golf match on TV in the clubhouse when an English guest came in and suggested turning up the sound a bit. 'Sshh! Not now, while Stephen Gallacher is putting!'

Scotland vs England

Jock was playing golf with the English minister of the local Piskie church. At the last hole, Jock missed a six-inch putt which cost him the match. Out of deference to his playing partner, he said absolutely nothing. The minister then observed, 'That was the most profane silence I have ever heard.'

MacTavish was watching a game of golf for the first time and was asked by a friend what he thought of the game. He replied, 'It looks to me like a harmless little ball chased by men too old to chase anything else.'

A Scotsman is shipwrecked and finally washes ashore on a small island. As he regains consciousness on the beach, he sees a beautiful unclad woman standing over him. She asks, 'Would you like some food?'

The Scot hoarsely croaks, 'Yes, please, I haven't eaten a bite of food for a week and I am very hungry.'

She disappears into the woods and quickly comes back with a basket of food.

When he has choked it down, she asks, 'Would you like something to drink?'

'Oh, yes, that food has made me very thirsty and I would very much like a drink!'

She goes off into the woods again and returns with a bottle of seventy-five-year-old single-malt whisky and a bottle of Highland Spring.

The Scotsman is beginning to think that he's in heaven when the unclad woman leans closer and says, 'Would you like to play around?'

'Oh, you beautiful darling sweet woman, don't tell me you've got a golf course here too!'

English golfer: 'Well, how do you like my game?'

St Andrews caddie: 'I suppose it's all right, but I still prefer golf.'

In the Highlands they tell the story of a minister who had been badly beaten at golf by a member of his congregation thirty years his senior.

'Cheer up,' his opponent said, as they returned to the clubhouse. 'Remember you win at the finish. You'll probably be burying me one of these days.'

'Even then,' replied the minister, 'it will be your hole.'

An Englishman was playing a golf course in Scotland and playing very badly. 'Dear Christ!' he remarked at last. 'There can't be worse players than me.'

'Well, well, maybe there are worse players,' commented the Scottish caddie, 'but they don't play.'

13, Unlucky for Some
Funnily Enough, Not Everyone
Likes England

England is the only country in the world where the food is more dangerous than the sex.

Jackie Mason

The English country gentleman galloping after the fox – the unspeakable in full pursuit of the uneatable.

Oscar Wilde

You should study the Peerage. It is the best thing in fiction the English have ever done.

Oscar Wilde

The English public takes no interest in a work of art until it is told that the work in question is immoral.

Oscar Wilde

The national sport of England is obstacle-racing. People fill their rooms with useless and cumbersome furniture, and spend the rest of their lives trying to dodge it.

Herbert Beerbohm Tree

The German originates it, the Frenchman imitates it and the Englishman exploits it.

German saying

To many, no doubt, he will seem blatant and bumptious, but we prefer to regard him as being simply English.

Oscar Wilde

If one could only teach the English how to talk, and the Irish how to listen, society here would be quite civilised.

Oscar Wilde

It is quite untrue that English people don't appreciate music. They may not understand it but they absolutely love the noise it makes.

Sir Thomas Beecham

Unmitigated noodles.

Kaiser Wilhelm II on England

Perfidious Albion.

French saying

I know why the sun never sets on the British Empire
– God would never trust an Englishman in the dark.
  Duncan Spaeth

The English think soap is civilisation.
  Heinrich von Treitschke

The Englishman who has lost his fortune is said to
have died of a broken heart.
  Ralph Waldo Emerson

There is one thing on earth more terrible than English
music, and that is English painting.
  Heinrich Heine

There are only two classes in good society in England:
the equestrian class and the neurotic class.
  George Bernard Shaw

England, the heart of a rabbit in the body of a lion.
The jaws of a serpent in an abode of popinjays.
  Eugene Deschamps

The English are not very spiritual people, so they
invented cricket to give them some idea of eternity.
  George Bernard Shaw

The way to endure summer in England is to have it framed and glazed in a comfortable room.
Horace Walpole

A pirate spreading misery and ruin over the face of the ocean.
Thomas Jefferson on England

An Englishman will burn his bed to catch a flea.
Turkish saying

What a pity it is that we have no amusements in England but vice and religion.
Sydney Smith

To learn English you must begin by thrusting the jaw forward, almost clenching the teeth, and practically immobilising the lips. In this way, the English produce the series of unpleasant little mews of which their language consists.
José Ortega y Gasset

The English have a miraculous power of turning wine into water.
Oscar Wilde

An Englishwoman's shoes look as if they have been made by someone who has often heard shoes described but has never seen any.

Anonymous

The average cooking in the average hotel for the average Englishman explains to a large extent the English bleakness and taciturnity. Nobody can beam and warble while chewing pressed beef smeared with diabolical mustard. Nobody can exult aloud while ungluing from his teeth a quivering tapioca pudding.

Karel Capek

English Law: where there are two alternatives: one intelligent, one stupid; one attractive, one vulgar; one noble, one ape-like; one serious and sincere, one undignified and false; one far-sighted, one short; everybody will invariably choose the latter.

Cyril Connolly

Poltroons, cowards, sulkers and dastards.

Eustache Deschamps

The English think that incompetence is the same thing as sincerity.

Quentin Crisp

We know of no spectacle so ridiculous as the British public in one of its periodical fits of morality.
Thomas Babington Macaulay

England is, after all, the land where children were beaten, wives and babies bashed, football hooligans crunch, and Miss Whip and Miss Lash ply their trade as nowhere else in the western world. Despite our belief that we are a 'gentle' people we have, in reality, a cruel and callous streak in our sweet natures, reinforced by a decadent puritan strain which makes some of us believe that suffering, whether useful or not, is a fit scourge to the wanton soul.
Colin MacInnes

If you live in Birmingham, then being awake is not necessarily a desirable state.
Tony Wilson

The English, who eat their meat red and bloody, show the savagery that goes with such food.
J.O. de la Mettrie

Continental people have a sex life; the English have hot-water bottles.
George Mikes

The English have no exalted sentiments. They can all be bought.

Napoleon

On a fine day the climate of England is like looking up a chimney, on a foul day it is like looking down.

Anonymous

We English are good at forgiving our enemies; it releases us from the obligation of liking our friends.

P.D. James

London, dirty little pool of life.

B.M. Malabari

Curse the blasted, jelly-boned swines, the slimy, the belly-wriggling invertebrates, the miserable sodding rotters, the flaming sods, the snivelling, dribbling, dithering, palsied, pulse-less lot that make up England today. They've got white of egg in their veins, and their spunk is that watery it's a marvel they can breed.

D.H. Lawrence

Freedom of discussion is in England little else than the right to write or say anything which a jury of twelve shopkeepers think it expedient should be said or written.

A.V. Dicey

All Englishmen talk as if they've got a bushel of plums stuck in their throats, and then after swallowing them get constipated from the pips.

W.C. Fields

The depressing thing about an Englishman's traditional love of animals is the dishonesty thereof ... Get a barbed hook into the upper lip of a salmon, drag him endlessly around the water until he loses his strength, pull him to the bank, hit him on the head with a stone, and you may well become fisherman of the year. Shoot the salmon and you'll never be asked again.

Clement Freud

It is only necessary to raise a bugbear before the English imagination in order to govern it at will. Whatever they hate or fear, they implicitly believe in, merely from the scope it gives to these passions.

William Hazlitt

A broad definition of crime in England is that it is any lower-class activity that is displeasing to the upper class.

David Frost and Anthony Jay

It is related of an Englishman that he hanged himself to avoid the daily task of dressing and undressing.

Johann Wolfgang von Goethe

The attitude of the English towards English history reminds one a good deal of the attitude of a Hollywood director towards love.

Margaret Halsey

A demon took a monkey to wife – the result by the grace of God was the English.

Indian saying

From every Englishman emanates a kind of gas, the deadly choke-damp of boredom.

Heinrich Heine

England has become a squalid, uncomfortable, ugly place . . . an intolerant, racist, homophobic, narrow-minded, authoritarian rat-hole run by vicious, suburban-minded, materialistic philistines.

Hanif Kureishi

The devil take these people and their language! They take a dozen monosyllabic words in their jaws, chew them, crunch them and spit them out again, and call that speaking. Fortunately they are by nature fairly silent, and although they gaze at us open-mouthed, they spare us long conversations.

Heinrich Heine

The English are ... perfidious and cunning, plotting the destruction of the lives of foreigners, so that even if they humbly bend the knee, they cannot be trusted.

Leo de Rozmital

A nation of ants, morose, frigid, and still preserving the same dread of happiness and joy as in the days of John Knox.

Max O'Rell

The perfidious, savage, disdainful, stupid, slothful, inhospitable, stupid English.

Julius Caesar Scaliger

An Englishman does everything on principle: he fights you on patriotic principles; he robs you on business principles; he enslaves you on imperial principles.

George Bernard Shaw

Englishmen never will be slaves; they are free to do whatever the government and public opinion allow them.
George Bernard Shaw

It must be acknowledged that the English are the most disagreeable of all the nations of Europe, more surly and morose, with less disposition to please, to exert themselves for the good of society, to make small sacrifices, and to put themselves out of their way.
Sydney Smith

The ordinary Britisher imagines that God is an Englishman.
George Bernard Shaw

The moment the very name of Scotland is mentioned, the English seem to bid adieu to common feeling, common prudence, and common sense, and to act with the barbarity of tyrants, and the fatuity of idiots.
Sydney Smith

The English take their pleasures sadly, after the fashion of their country.
Maximilien de Béthune

The two sides of industry have traditionally always regarded each other in England with the greatest possible loathing, mistrust and contempt. They are both absolutely right.

Auberon Waugh

To disagree with three-fourths of the English public on all points is one of the first elements of sanity, one of the deepest consolations in all moments of spiritual doubt.

Oscar Wilde

In England it is enough for a man to try and produce any serious, beautiful work to lose all his rights as a citizen.

Oscar Wilde

Thinking is the most unhealthy thing in the world, and people die of it just as they die of any other disease. Fortunately, in England at any rate, thought is not catching.

Oscar Wilde

Englishmen are babes in philosophy and so prefer faction-fighting to the labour of its unfamiliar thought.

W.B. Yeats

14
Damn Few and They're A' Deid

The average Englishman, in the home he calls his castle, slips into his national costume – a shabby raincoat, patented by chemist Charles Macintosh from Glasgow, Scotland.

En route to his office he strides along the English lane, surfaced by John Macadam of Ayr, Scotland.

He drives an English car fitted with tyres invented by John Boyd Dunlop of Dreghorn, Scotland.

At the office he receives the mail, which bears adhesive stamps invented by James Chalmers of Dundee, Scotland.

During the day he uses the telephone invented by Alexander Graham Bell, born in Edinburgh, Scotland.

At home in the evening his daughter pedals her bicycle, invented by Kirkpatrick Macmillan, a blacksmith of Dumfries, Scotland.

He watches the news on TV, an invention of John Logie Baird of Helensburgh, Scotland, and hears an item about the US Navy, founded by John Paul Jones of Kirkbean, Scotland.

He has by now been reminded too much of Scotland and in desperation he picks up the Bible, only to find that the first man mentioned in the good book is a Scot – King James VI, who authorised its translation.

Nowhere can an Englishman turn to escape the ingenuity of the Scots.

He could take to drink, but the Scots make the best in the world.

He could take a rifle and end it all, but the breech-loading rifle was invented by Captain Patrick Ferguson of Pitfours, Scotland.

If he escaped death, he could find himself on an operating table injected with penicillin, discovered by Alexander Fleming of Darvel, Scotland, and given an anaesthetic, discovered by Sir James Young Simpson of Bathgate, Scotland.

Out of the anaesthetic he would find no comfort in learning that he was as safe as the Bank of England, founded by William Paterson of Dumfries, Scotland.

Perhaps his only remaining hope would be to get a transfusion of Scottish blood, which would entitle him to ask, 'WHA'S LIKE US?'

Being Scottish is about driving in a German car to an Irish pub for a Belgian beer, then travelling home, grabbing an Indian curry or a Turkish kebab on the way, to sit on Swedish furniture and watch American shows on a Japanese TV.

And the most Scottish thing of all? Suspicion of all things foreign!

Only in Scotland can a pizza get to your house faster than an ambulance.

Only in Scotland do supermarkets make sick people walk all the way to the back of the shop to get their prescriptions while healthy people can buy cigarettes at the front.

Only in Scotland do people order double cheese-burgers, large fries and a DIET coke.

Only in Scotland do banks leave both doors open and chain the pens to the counters.

Only in Scotland do we leave cars worth thousands of pounds on the drive and lock our junk and cheap lawnmower in the garage.

Only in Scotland do we use answering machines to screen calls and then have call waiting so we won't miss a call from someone we didn't want to talk to in the first place.

Only in Scotland are there disabled parking places in front of a skating rink.

Not to mention:

Three Scots die each year by testing if a 9v battery works with their tongue.

In 2012, 142 Scots were injured by not removing all pins from new shirts.

Fifty-eight Scots are injured each year by using sharp knives instead of screwdrivers.

Thirty-one Scots have died since 2009 by watering their Christmas tree while the fairy lights were plugged in.

Nineteen Scots have died in the last three years believing that Christmas decorations were chocolate.

Scottish Hospitals reported four broken arms last year after Christmas-cracker-pulling accidents.

Eighteen Scots had serious burns in 2013 trying on a new jumper with a lit cigarette in their mouth.

A massive 543 Scots have been admitted to A&E in

the last two years after trying to open bottles of beer with their teeth.

Five Scots were injured last year in accidents involving out-of-control Scalextric cars.

And finally ...

In 2013, eight Scots were admitted to hospital with fractured skulls incurred whilst throwing up into the toilet.

SCOTLAND: wha is like us indeed?

15
For, Against and In Between

The truth of the matter is that we Scots have always been more divided amongst ourselves than pitted against the English. Scottish history before the Union of the Parliaments is a gloomy, violent tale of murders, feuds and tribal revenge. Only after the Act of Union did Highlanders and Lowlanders, Picts and Celts, begin to recognise one another as fellow citizens.

Tam Dalyell, Labour politician, MP for West Lothian (1962–83) and for Linlithgow (1983–2005)

Thank you for uniting us, nice English people. Now could you fuck off?

Ian Black, freelance scribbler

Nowhere beats the heart so kindly as beneath the tartan plaid.

W.E. Aytoun

Where is the coward that would not dare to fight for such a land as Scotland?

Sir Walter Scott

People imagine we Scots are all red-haired and about five feet small. I reckon there's no race more romantic than the Scots.

Sean Connery

That old lonely lovely way of living in Highland places – twenty years a-growing, twenty years flowering, twenty years declining – father to son, mother to daughter giving rich tradition; peaceful bounty flowing; one harmony, all tones of life combining – old, wise ways, passed like the dust blowing.

Douglas Young

> In the highlands, in the country places,
> Where the old men have rosy faces,
> And the young maidens
> Quiet eyes.
>
> *Robert Louis Stevenson*

Never Ignore the Fiery Cross

When a chieftain wished to summon members of his clan in an emergency, he killed a goat. Next he made a cross of light wood, burned its extremities in the fire, then extinguished the flames in the animal's blood. This was called the Fiery Cross – also *Creau Toigh* or the Cross of Shame because disobedience to what the symbol implied incurred infamy. The cross was transferred from hand to hand and sped through the chief's lands with incredible speed. At the sight of the cross, every man, from sixteen to sixty, was obliged to go to the appointed meeting place. Anyone who ignored the summons was exposed to the penalties of fire and sword, which were denoted by the bloody and burned marks on the cross.

If we had had email, we would probably never have joined the Union and the Stuarts would still be on the throne of Scotland.

You talked of Scotland as a lost cause and that is not true. Scotland is an unwon cause.
John Steinbeck (letter to Mrs John F. Kennedy)

God help England if she had no Scots to think for her.
George Bernard Shaw

That Scotland is a part of the United Kingdom is an almost inevitable accident: at the same time, the unity of the English and the Scots should never be assumed. It was Sir Walter Scott who pointed out that the Scots and the English had fought three hundred and fourteen major battles against one another before their Union; this kind of historical animosity does not disappear overnight. The fact remains that the two countries are altogether distinct in temperament and manner, and their conjunction, although it is by now a working one, has never been resolved to the satisfaction of either.

*Alastair Reid (*The New Yorker, *1964)*

What motivated me was that I wanted to hear the Scottish anthem, I wanted to see the Scottish flag flying and I wanted to be up there on the rostrum. When it happened, it was the most special moment of my career so far.

Yvonne Murray (after winning her gold medal in the 10,000 metres at the Commonwealth Games in Canada)

The Scots hate the Union but they hate each other more.

Daniel Defoe

This is my country
The land that begat me,
These windy spaces
Are surely my own.
And those who here toil
In the sweat of their faces
Are flesh of my flesh
And bone of my bone.
Sir Alexander Gray, 'Scotland'

The proper drinking of Scotch whisky is more than indulgence: it is a toast to civilisation, a tribute to the continuity of culture, a manifesto of man's determination to use the resources of nature to refresh mind and body and enjoy to the full the senses with which he has been endowed.

David Daiches, Scotch Whisky *(1969)*

There's nae power on earth can crush the men that can sing.

Joe Corrie

It is noteworthy that the nobles of the country [Scotland] have maintained a quite despicable behaviour since the days of Wallace downwards – a selfish, ferocious, famishing, unprincipled set of hyenas, from whom at no time, and in no way, has the country derived any benefit whatever.

Thomas Carlyle

But I am half a Scot by birth, and bred
A whole one, and my heart flies to my head
As Auld Lang Syne brings Scotland, one and all
Scotch plaids, Scotch snoods, the blue hills,
and clear streams,
The Dee, the Don, Balgounie's Brig's
black wall,

Scotland vs England

All my boy feelings, all my gentler dreams
Of what I then dreamt, clothed in their own pall,
Like Banqo's offspring. Floating past me seems
My childhood in this childishness of mine;
I care not – 'tis a glimpse of Auld Lang Syne.

George Gordon Byron, 6th Baron Byron,
from Don Juan

The Lord in his wisdom gave us the Cheviots as a defensive barrier. We really needed the Alps.
W. Oliver Brown

While Scotland became North Britain, England never became South Britain.
W. Oliver Brown

The real romance of the '45 was not the charm of the Prince but the morality of the people who were not tempted by the £30,000 which any of them could have claimed for betraying him. The statue at Glenfinnan is not to honour Prince Charlie – but the men who fought and died for him.
W. Oliver Brown

I am one of those who always think it is fun to be in Scotland.
Joseph Hilaire Pierre René Belloc

What do philosophers call the truth?

When one Scottish fisherman calls another Scots fisherman a liar.

Anonymous

The three finest sights in the world – a field of ripe wheat, a ship in full sail, and the wife of a MacDonald with child.

Anonymous

The Scots – a race unconquered, by her climate made bold.

Anonymous

The Scot has never been very servile or 'supple at the knee', and it has always been one of his striking characteristics to regard independence as the first of earthly blessings. His love of liberty has never been subdued. The past has taught him to stand firmly on his own legs and to look the world steadily in the eye. He has 'a very good conceit of himself' and is quick to resent rebuke or even the mildest criticism.

Anonymous

When do you think the following was written?

Long ago, it is said, the people of Athens were asked to record two votes, one for the best man in the State, the man most suited for high position in respect to character, ability, energy and so forth, and the second vote for the second best. The citizens all voted, we are told, each giving the first place to himself, as the cleverest and most trustworthy man in the State. But the second votes were all registered for Themistocles, who thus came victoriously into office.

Something like this would very likely happen if the inhabitants of all civilised countries were invited to name what they deemed the best land to be born in; and were to give another vote to decide which was the second best.

We ought all to give our suffrages for our own country first. That would be only fair and right. Anything short of that would savour of lack of patriotism on our part. But no doubt the great majority of people would agree to accord Scotland the second vote, which would bring in the Land of Cakes at the head of the poll.

And yet, is Scotland so exceedingly popular? Yes, and No. Occasionally people here and there awaken to the 'pervasiveness' of Scotland, and write to the papers. Quite recently someone discovered that all holders of high office in England but six were connected with North-Britain. Then someone else wrote to the *Times* that these six were of Scottish descent or were married to Scotswomen.

Objection is sometimes taken to the Scot as being masterful and enterprising, that he is always found, as they put it: 'carrying on the affairs of the Empire.' That phrase expresses a mysterious principle which has been at work for centuries. If ever you see an enterprise specially successful anywhere 'a going concern', no matter where, in Tibet, or Peru, or at the sources of the Nile, there is certain to be a gentleman from North of the Tweed at the helm of affairs. In politics, or law, in commerce, or in science it is just the same.

Other nationalities – English, Welsh, Irish, get a look in now and then; still for the actual working of any money-making business you will find matters entrusted either to a Lowlander or a Highlander, but assuredly to some kind of a Scot.

A. G. Gardiner, the author of those lively sketches 'Prophets, Priests and Kings', of some years ago was scarcely exaggerating when he said:

To be born a Scotsman is to be born with a silver spoon in the mouth. It is to be born, as it were, into the governing family. We English are the hewers of wood and drawers of water for our Caledonian masters. Formerly they used to raid our borders and steal our cattle, but they kept to their own soil. In those happy days an Englishman had a chance in his own country. Today he is little better than a hod carrier. The Scotsmen have captured not our cattle, but the British Empire. They sit in the seats of the mighty. Westminster is their washpot, and over Canada do they cast out their shoe. The head of the English Church is a Scotsman, and his brother of York came out of a Scotch Presbyterian manse. The Premier is usually a Scotsman and, if not Scotch, he sits for a Scotch constituency, and the Lord Chancellor, the keeper of the King's conscience, is a Scotsman too.

London has become an annexe of Edinburgh, and Canada is little more than a Scotch off-hand farm. Our single satisfaction is that whenever we want a book to read we have only to apply to Skibo Castle and Mr. Carnegie will send a free library by return. It is a pleasant way he has of reminding us that we want educating.

Underneath this playful badinage there lurks a great deal of truth. The details are, of course, a trifle out of date at the moment, but the principle holds. When Tammas Buchanan returned from a week's stay in London, whither he had been sent by his firm to carry out some delicate business negotiations, the neighbours were eager to know what he thought of the people in the South. 'Tell us, Tammas, hoo did ye fin' the English? What like warr' they, noo?'

'English!' exclaimed Tammas. 'Mon, Ah dinna ken onything about them. Ah had naething to do with the English. Ah only had to deal with the heids o' the departments.'

Cuey-Na-Gael, Scots Humour and Heroism *(1902)*

Things haven't changed a lot in the intervening century or so since this was written, have they?

16
Kilts and the Kiddin'

'A Jock in a frock with a knife in his sock' was a description passed by an English chap to his mate when they found themselves in company in a pub with a pipe band after a competition in Canada.

It took them days to recover enough of the body to bury him.

Why do Scotsmen wear kilts?

Because the sheep got used to the sound of zips.

The kilt is an unrivalled garment for fornication and diarrhoea.

Why do they call it a 'kilt'?

Because a lot of English people get kilt when they call it a skirt.

How do you tell Scottish women from Scottish men, since they both wear kilts?

The one listening is the man.

Safer in the Kilt

A new (British) safety report confirms what every real Scot knows. Donning the kilt instead of trousers is good for your health. The Department of Trade and Industry determined that putting on trousers poses a serious risk of injury because people lose their balance and topple over, hurting themselves. The critical and most dangerous part is pulling up the second leg when the first is still at half-mast. The yearly home accident report by the DTI estimates there were 4,400 trouser victims last year. Another 400 injured themselves putting on their underwear.

Kiltmaker Gordon Nicholson of McCalls of Edinburgh seized on the report as evidence of what he has been preaching for years. He said: 'If people would only wear traditional costume, all this pain and injury would be prevented. I have never heard of anyone injuring themselves putting on a kilt. I've heard of people injuring themselves once they've got it on,' he added. 'I would think if there were any injuries linked to kilts then they would be from dancing or drinking.'

Scot Whips Off His Kilt to Save a Man's Life

A Scotsman saved the life of a stranded hillwalker on a remote mountainside by taking off his kilt and wrapping it round the shivering man. Bare-bottomed Andy Young, forty-three, braved the elements as he stripped down and used his kilt and thick cotton shirt to keep the hypothermic man warm. Mr Young cuddled close to Tom Mitchell, forty-one, and sang him traditional Scottish songs while they waited two hours on chilly Sron Ghorm, near the Aultguish Inn, Wester Ross, for a helicopter. Mr Mitchell, of Collynie, Methlick, near Aberdeen, had gone for a lone hill walk on Monday but did not return to the inn. Friends were particularly concerned because he was epileptic.

Mr Young said, 'It was all I could think of because he was shivering so much. I cuddled in close beside him and I think our body heat kept us alive. I sang songs to him to keep his spirits up. I sang "MacPherson's" Rant, the "Skye Boat Song" and "Pittenweem Joe" over and over again. When the helicopter arrived, I took my kilt and shirt back and looked on as he was winched into the helicopter. I did not want to have to walk into the inn naked.'

You could have, Andy. You did us proud.

During a recent international sports competition, one of the Scottish track and field coaches was entertaining friends and colleagues in his hotel room. As so often occurs, the libations were used up before it was time to end the festivities. After receiving directions to the nearest offie, the Scottish coach left the party to bring back more booze. Arriving at the store, he noticed there were two men waiting in the queue. Both were dressed in olive-drab military fatigues, had heavy beards, and cigars in their mouths. He heard the first one order several bottles of various liquors. Upon being told the cost of his purchases, the individual told the proprietor that he was with 'the Cubans'. The salesman produced a book and had him sign for his purchases. The other individual proceeded to order at least twice the amount of his companion. Upon receipt of his total, he also told the clerk that he was with 'the Cubans'.

By now, the Scot figured he was on to a very good thing. He ordered numerous bottles of various boozes, cigars, cigarettes et cetera. Upon being presented with his total, he said that he too was with 'the Cubans'. The proprietor replied that he could not be with the Cubans.

'And why not?' demanded the indignant Scotsman.

'Because you don't have a beard and a large Cuban cigar,' the proprietor replied.

At that, the Scot reached down, lifted his kilt and proclaimed, 'Secret Service!'

And, of course, there is a response to the most asked question: 'Is anything worn under your kilt?' The standard reply is, 'No. Everything is in perfect working order.'

Here are a few more possible replies to that perennial query:

'Brogues and stockings.'

'My Scottish pride.'

'How warm are your hands?'

'Play your cards right and you can find out.'

'My mother once told me a real lady wouldn't ask. She was right.'

'Tell me, madam, would you go jogging without a bra?'

To another man: 'Same as you, only bigger.'

To another man: 'Your wife's/sister's/mother's lipstick.'

To a woman: 'If I'm lucky, your lipstick.'

'Lipstick – two shades on a good day!'

'Socks, shoes and a wee bit of talcum powder.'

'Bagpipes. Want to give them a blow?'

By a man: 'A wee set of pipes.'

By a man: 'String. I had to tie it up so it didn't hang below the kilt.'

By a man: 'It's the smallest airport in the world – two hangars and a night fighter.'

By a woman: 'A wee sporran.'

By a woman: 'Chanel No. 5.'

'How badly do you want to know?'

To a woman at church: 'What God graced me with.'

'Gie's your hand, lassie, I'm a man of few words.'

'Bare essentials.'

17
Republicans 'R' Us

Young McGregor rushed into a church, placed his broadsword under a pew and entered the confessional. 'Father,' he said breathlessly, 'I've just killed two English redcoats.' Hearing no response, he went on. 'I also did for their captain!' When there was still no response from the priest, McGregor said, 'Father, have ye fainted?'

'Of course I haven't fainted,' replied the confessor. 'I'm waiting for you to stop talking politics and commence confessing your sins.'

18
The Pipes Are Calling

Bagpipes: The Missing Link Between Music and Noise

Twelve clansmen and one bagpipe make a rebellion.
  Sir Walter Scott

Some men there are love not a gaping pig; some that are mad if they behold a cat; and others, when the bagpipe sings . . . cannot contain their urine.
  William Shakespeare

I enjoy them best from a great distance.
  Anonymous

The inventor of the bagpipes was inspired when he saw a man carrying an asthmatic pig under his arm. Unfortunately, the man-made object never equalled the purity of sound achieved by the pig.
  Alfred Hitchcock

They say that he [Nero] can play the aulos both with his mouth, and also with the armpit, a bag being thrown under it.

Dio Chrysostom

They only have nine notes. Just how difficult could the pipes be to learn?

Aspiring piper

What are these men going to do with such bundles of sticks? I can supply them with better implements of war.

Duke of Cumberland, reviewing Highlanders in his employ (1745)

Music they [the Scots] have, but not the harmony of the spheres, but loud taurean noises, like the bellowing of beasts.

Englishman (1679)

Thank God there is no odour.

Oscar Wilde

'There's meat and music here,' said the fox as he ran off with the bagpipes.

Scottish axiom

Give the piper a penny to play and two pence to leave.
  English proverb

He screw'd the pipes and mak'd them skirl, till roof an'
rafters aw' did dirl.
  Robert Burns

The best things written about the bagpipe are written
on five lines of the great staff.
  Pipe Major Donald MacLeod, MBE

If thy neighbour offend thee, give each of his children
bagpipes.
  Scottish proverb

Out of the houses the rats came tumbling
Great rats, small rats, lean rats, brawny rats
Followed the Piper for their lives.
  Robert Browning, 'The Pied Piper of Hamelin' *(1842)*

Golf is a game invented by the same people who think
music comes out of a bagpipe.
  Anonymous

But canna get oot a richt note, for the bubblyjock swallowed the bagpipes. And the blether stuck in its throat.

Hugh MacDiarmid

Many of them were Scotchmen in their plaids and their music was delightful. Even the bagpipe was not disagreeable.

John Adams, US President

Yon squakin' saxophone gives me the syncopated gripes.

I'm sick of jazz, I want to hear the skirling of the pipes.

Robert Service, poet

Ancient Piping Joke

The lads are marching into battle, with the piper playing away like mad. The enemy's arrows, swords and spears are creating bloody slaughter throughout the Scottish ranks.

Ten men down and the piper plays on. Twenty men down and still the pipes skirl out. Finally fifty men have fallen and the chieftain says to the piper, 'For Christ's sake, Angus, can you not play something they like?'

Why do pipers have such large families?

Their wives will do ANYTHING to get them to stop playing.

What's the difference between a piper and a pension fund?

The fund eventually matures and earns money.

How can you tell when bagpipes are out of tune?

Someone's blowing them.

What's the difference between bagpipe music and a bucket of shite?

The bucket.

Why do pipe bands tour so often?

It keeps assassins guessing.

What's one thing you never hear people say?

Oh, that's the bagpiper's Porsche.

What's the difference between a Scotsman and a Rolling Stone?

A Rolling Stone says, 'Hey, you, get off of my cloud!' while a Scotsman says, 'Hey, McLeod, get off of my ewe!'

How is playing the bagpipes like throwing a javelin blindfolded?

You don't have to be very good to get people's attention.

In a recent newsflash it was announced that terrorists have taken ninety pipe bands hostage. If their demands aren't met they'll release one every hour.

Pipers' T-shirts

Eat, sleep, pipe. What else is there?

Bagpipes: putting the FUN back in FUNeral.

Bagpipes: not just for funerals any more.

Piobaireachd. If you can't say it, you can't play it.

Piper – is that a problem, pal?

Here, Nessie, Nessie, Nessie!

I don't SUFFER from insanity. I ENJOY every minute of it.

Scottish Hot Air Balloon.

Scottish Windbag.

I'm full of hot air.

And finally, the deeply, deeply worrying:
Bagpipes: Not just for Scots any more.

19
See Us? See Dry? See Deserts

It has been rightly said that there are as many sides to the Scottish character as there are checks in a tartan. In moving about his world, he is concerned primarily with the practical use of things. When Sandy was shown St Paul's for the first time, his only comment was, 'Man, it would hold a terrible lot of hay.' And when the Lord Provost of a major Scottish city was asked to express an opinion about the Pyramids, his summing up was: 'What a lot of masonry work and no rent coming in.' Show a Scot the majesty of the Eiffel Tower, and he asks, 'What fool built that thing?' Put him down on the banks of Niagara and his main concern is for the 'perfect waste of water'.

There is a pungency and penetration in much of our humour, confirming that first and last we are realists, with a good grip on fact, and dryness is part of it.

'And how is your new minister getting on?' the villager was asked.

'Oh, fine, I think,' was the reply, 'but he's hardly settled in yet.'

'But they tell me he is one of the kind that doesn't believe in hell.'

'Well,' came the rejoinder, 'he'll not be here all that long before he changes his mind.'

The day of the funeral had come and gone and the old widow was receiving a visit of condolence from some of her friends in the village, who were reminding her that life was indeed brief.

'It's just the way of the world, Mrs McKay,' said one of them with some word of comfort.

'Here today and gone tomorrow,' was the reply, 'just like the circus.'

Andrew had been busy for a long time in clearing some very rough ground as an extension to his croft. After months of toil, he was at last seeing some of the fruits of his labours and, with pardonable pride, was admiring the display of blooms and vegetables when the minister approached with a smile of approval.

'Well, Andrew,' he began, 'I must say that you and the Creator have, between you, done a grand job on this ground.'

But Andrew was not too pleased about the division of credit. 'Maybe so,' he replied, 'maybe so, but you should have seen it when the Creator had it all to Himself.'

One day, young Willie was making very poor progress with his rice pudding and his mother was doing all she could to encourage him to empty his plate. As a final inducement, she reminded him that in China there were millions and millions of children who would be thankful for even a small plate of rice.

But the matter-of-fact Willie was not yet convinced. 'Well,' he challenged, 'name one.'

Sandy was on his way home late one night when a neighbour beckoned him for help. 'Here,' he said, 'give me a hand to get this pig out of the truck.'

When they had got the pig out of his truck, the neighbour said, 'Hold the pig still while I open the front door.' Sandy did as he was told and the neighbour said, 'Now help me push the pig upstairs.' Sandy did that. 'Now,' said the neighbour, 'help me put the pig in the bath.' After a great deal of effort they managed to put the pig in the bath.

'Look,' said Sandy, 'what is going on here? Why do you need to put a huge pig in the bath?'

'I suppose you're entitled to an explanation,' said the neighbour. 'You see, the problem is with my wife: she's English and she's one of those women who always knows everything. No matter what I tell her, she says, "I know, I know."'

'But how is a pig in the bath going to help?' asked Sandy.

'Well, tomorrow morning,' said the neighbour, 'she's going to rush into the bedroom and scream at me, "There's a huge pig in the bath!" and I'm going to lie back in bed and say to her, "I know, I know."'

Maggie was an old maid. One early spring day, Maggie was out shopping and a beautiful red wool suit caught her attention. Rushing inside the shop, she asked, 'Do you have another of those red wool suits like the one I saw from outside in the window?'

'Yes, madam,' the saleswoman began. 'Wait here and I'll make sure.'

Shortly, the woman returned and Maggie's ear-to-ear smile said she was bound to make a purchase within minutes.

'Can I try it on?' asked Maggie.

The woman handed the suit to Maggie and showed her to the dressing room. In seconds, Maggie was back and admiring herself in the nice red wool suit in the closest mirror.

'May I wrap it for you or do you wish to wear it?' asked the woman.

'Oh,' said Maggie, 'I forgot to ask. What's the price? How much are you asking for it?'

'It's £549.95,' the woman answered.

'I do not believe it,' said Maggie, as she rushed back to the dressing area to take off the suit. 'I am not going to pay that much for one wool suit!' Soon, she was dressed and out of the shop.

A little while later in the shopping centre, Maggie spotted another suit that looked exactly like the one she had tried on at the first store. This time, her first question was about the price of the red wool suit. Upon learning the price and checking it out to prove to herself that it was indeed the same suit at a much better price, Maggie paid for the new suit and, with it neatly boxed and under her arm, she rushed back to the first store.

'Hello,' Maggie shouted when she spotted the woman who tried to sell her the overpriced same suit. 'Look what I found in another dress shop, and it only cost me £49.95!'

'Yes,' the woman said, 'but this is not the same suit. The one you tried on here is made of virgin wool.'

Maggie thought about that momentarily and said, 'I saved £500.00. What the fuck do I care what the sheep do at night?'

David Cameron called George, né Gideon, Osborne into his office one day and said, 'George, I have a great idea! We are going to go all out to win back Middle England.'

'Good idea, PM. How will we go about it?' said Osborne.

'Well,' said Cameron, 'we'll get ourselves two of those long Barbour coats, some proper wellies, a stick and a flat cap – oh, and a Labrador. Then we'll really look the part. We'll go to a nice old country pub in Durrington, Wiltshire, and we'll show them that we really enjoy the countryside.'

'Right, PM,' said Osborne. So a few days later, all kitted out and with the requisite Labrador at heel, they set off from London in a westerly direction. Eventually they arrived at just the place they were looking for and found a lovely pub and, with the dog, went in and up to the bar.

'Good evening, landlord, might we have two pints of your best ale, from the wood?' said Cameron.

'Good evening, Prime Minister,' said the landlord. 'Two pints of best it is, coming up.'

Cameron and Osborne stood leaning on the bar drinking their beer and chatting, nodding now and again to those who came into the bar for a drink. The dog lay quietly at their feet.

All of a sudden, the door from the adjacent bar opened and in came a grizzled old shepherd, complete with crook. He walked up to the Labrador, lifted its tail and looked underneath, shrugged his shoulders and walked back to the other bar. A few moments later, in came another old shepherd with his crook. He walked up to the dog, lifted its tail, looked underneath, scratched his head and went back to the other bar. Over the course of the next hour or so, another four or five shepherds came in, lifted the dog's tail and went away looking puzzled.

Eventually Cameron and Osborne could stand it no longer and called the barman over. 'Tell me,' said Cameron, 'why did all those old shepherds come in and look under the dog's tail like that? Is it an old custom?'

'Good lord, no,' said the barman. 'It's just that someone has told them that there was a Labrador in this bar with two arseholes.'

There was a survey commissioned on the accepted way of shagging a sheep and in most of Scotland, large parts of England, and all of Wales the consensus was that you did it from the back with their back legs down your wellies. Except, apparently, in Dumfries-shire, where they do it from the front. So they sent Bob Wyllie and a BBC film crew down to Moniaive to investigate. Here is a transcript of big Bob's first interview:

> BW: I'm here in Moniaive to find out what it is that makes the Dumfriesshire sheep-shagging method so radically different from the rest of

the country. I'm going to stop this country gentleman and ask him. Excuse me, sir, do you shag sheep?

CG: Aye, ah dae. Ah dae that, aye, sheep, aye.

BW: And can I ask you, what position do you use?

CG: Aye, ah suppose it's a bit like the missionary position. Ye grab the sheep, tummle it ower oan its back, climb oan tae its belly an' fling yer nidger intae it – aye, so ye dae, ye fling yer nidger right up it.

BW: That's fascinating. Did you know that, in the rest of the country, they do it from the back?

CG: Aye, ah dae, Ah know that but it's no' sae good yon wey, ken.

BW: And why is that?

CG: Well, if ye dae it thon wey, ye miss oot oan aw the kissin'.

He's Still in Guantanamo Bay

An English chap is up in front of the court in Scotland, as so many of them are, for a wildlife offence – specifically, stealing the eggs of a red kite and killing and eating their mum.

Everything proceeds in a vaguely civilised fashion and the judge hands out a relatively lenient sentence.

As the man is led away, the judge asks him, 'Just out of curiosity, what did it taste like, the red kite?'

'Well, Your Honour,' said the Englishman, 'it's pretty much like golden eagle.'

Two young English lads are on a trip round Scotland when they pull over into a lay-by and pass their lunchtime watching some sheep. Just as they are finishing up a farmer appears in the field, grabs a sheep, sticks its head in the fence, ups with his kilt, shags the wee thing and walks away, leaving the sheep stuck in the fence.

The two boys have watched this in silence, then one turns to the other and says, 'What d'yer think, Cyril, fancy some of that?'

Cyril looks thoughtful and says, 'I wouldn't mind at all, mucker – wouldn't say no, but I'm not sure if I can get my head through the fence.'

An English Sunday School teacher was testing the children in her Scottish class to see if they understood the concept of getting to heaven.

She asked them, 'If I sold my house and my car, had a big house sale and gave all my money to the church, would that get me into heaven?'

'NO!' the children answered.

'If I cleaned the church every day, mowed the

garden, and kept everything neat and tidy, would that get me into heaven?'

Again, the answer was, 'NO!' By now she was starting to smile.

'Well, then, if I was kind to animals and gave sweets to all the children, and loved my husband would that get me into heaven?' she asked them again.

Again, they all answered, 'NO!'

'Well,' she continued, 'then how can I get into heaven?'

A six-year-old Weegie shouted: 'YOU'VE GOAT TAE BE FUCKIN' DEID.'

20
Fitba' and the English Bams

Findlay Hickey, a multi-re-upped Tartan Army footsoldier, wrote this a few years back and the sentiments, and the England supporters, don't seem to have changed much. The usual pint of choice to Findlay for allowing me to use it. An English chap named Coward might have had something to do with the tune.

Don't Let's Be Beastly to the English

Don't let's be beastly to the English,
When the Cup is ultimately won.
It was just those nasty tabloids
That encouraged them to fight,
And all their pomp and circumstance
Is far worse than its bite.
Let's be meek to them
And turn the other cheek to them
And try to bring out their latent sense of fun.
Let's give them what they think they're due
And say we wish they'd battled through,
But don't let's be beastly to the scum.

Fitba' and the English Bams

We must be kind, and with an open mind,
We must endeavour to play the game,
To let the English know that when the fighting's over
They were not the ones who were to blame.
We must be sweet, and tactful and discreet,
And when they've suffered defeat,
We mustn't let them feel upset,
Or ever get the feeling that we're cross with them or
hate them,
Our future policy must be to never bait them.

Don't let's be beastly to the English,
For *Schadenfreude* it really isn't done,
Let us treat them very kindly
As we would a valued friend,
And strong supportive shoulders to the vanquished
we must lend.
Let's be sweet to them and day by day repeat to them
That hooliganism simply isn't done.
Let's help the filthy clowns again
To smash up foreign towns again,
But don't let's be beastly to the scum.

We must be just and win their love and trust
And in addition we must be wise,
And ask the smashed-up towns to help us to applaud
them,

Scotland vs England

That would be a wonderful surprise!
For many years, they've been in floods of tears,
Because the poor little dears
Have been so wronged and only longed
To cheat the world, deplete the world and beat the
world to blazes,
This is the moment when we ought to sing their
praises.

Don't let's be beastly to the English,
For you can't deprive a bully of his fun.
Though they were a little naughty in the city of
Marseilles,
It would have been unkind to keep the rascals from
their play.
Let's be free with them and give up the BBC to them,
We mustn't prevent them basking in the sun.
Let's soften their defeat again
And let them have a bleat again,
But don't let's be beastly to the scum.

Don't let's be beastly to the English,
When another sporting season has begun.
We must send them our best wishes,
Give them all the cheer they need,
For an English fan's intentions can be always
guaranteed.

Let's accede to them and all our sport concede to
them,
They're better than us at honest manly fun.
Let's let them feel as swell again
And bore us all to hell again,
But don't let's be beastly to the scum.

Maybe it is just the way they say things, like:

'IF IT WASN'T FOR THE ENGLISH YOU'D BE
KRAUTS.'

In at No. 2 and to the same tune, the old party
favourite: 'I'D RATHER BE A PAKI THAN A
TURK.'

And where would we be without 'NO SURRENDER
TO THE IRA'?

Last, but not least, for the benefit of younger Germans,
'WE WON THE WAR, WE WON THE WAR, EE-
AYE-ADDIO, WE WON THE WAR.'

And they wonder why people pick on them.

21
In Which Our Southern Cousins Get Their Say

Yes, here he comes, the well-balanced Scot, a chip on each shoulder (or is that two deep-fried Mars Bars?), well-thumbed copy of the Barnett formula under his arm, genetically imprinted scowl, tattered kilt hanging below his knees and, yuck, no underwear. What are we to make of him (or her, to which all of the above also apply) as we approach the umpteenth anniversary of when the Scotch were welcomed into the mighty union of civilisations that is England (oops, Britain) and given the same chance to rape the planet and its indigenous civilisations as we were?

Not much, we would suggest, as we have been trying to teach you the mainstays of our empire-winning ways – these being public schools, snobbery and greed – for the last three centuries and the only place that has got the point – and that, just a little – is Edinburgh. The rest of you are just hopeless.

Of course, we don't want you to secede from the Union – at least not while there is still some oil left. After that runs out, you can bugger off. You won't need to erect any barriers at the border, incidentally, as we will be doing that anyway. These will be manned by Bulgarians and Romanians, our new source of cheap labour (sorry, friends and allies, unless UKIP wins a lot of seats at the next election). And don't be trying any of your knavish Jocko sweaty socko tricks, like befriending them or being nice to them, as their officers will all be products of our public school system and well used to the application of harsh and unbending cruelty.

Rest assured, though, if the Union does come to an end, that it hasn't been all bad and remember, in the words of the old country song, 'If I had to do it all over again, I'd do it all over you.'

Thanks for the oil and all the fish.

22
Let's Get the Mean Jock Bastards Bit Out of the Way

Rigid economy – a dead Scotsman.

It is said that all Scots have a sense of humour because it is a free gift.

An Englishman, an Irishman and a Scot went to a pub together.

The Englishman stood a round, the Irishman stood a round and the Scot stood around.

And then there was the Scotsman who bought only one spur. His thinking was that, if one side of the horse went, the other was sure to follow.

'It was like this,' said Donald. 'I was teaching the wife to drive and the brakes failed when we came down the hill.'

'What did you tell her?'

'Try and hit something cheap.'

Wedding guest: 'This is your fourth daughter to get married, isn't it?'

MacDonald: 'Aye. Our confetti is getting awfy dirty.'

A Scotsman's ideal holiday is to stay at home and let his mind wander.

It was a terrible winter – three months of unbroken blizzards. McTavish hadn't been seen in the village for weeks, so a Red Cross rescue team struggled to his remote croft at the head of the glen. It was completely buried – only the chimney was showing.

'McTavish,' they shouted down the chimney. 'Are you there?'

'Wha's that?' came the answer.

'It's the Red Cross,' they called.

'Go away,' shouted McTavish. 'I bought a flag last year!'

A Scot at a garage: 'I want a pint of petrol and a cup of oil.'

Scottish petrol-pump attendant: 'Do you want me to cough into the tyres as well?'

An Edinburgh salesman died in a tragic car accident while travelling for his company over the winding roads of the Highlands. His manager sent the following telegram: 'RETURN SAMPLES BY 2ND CLASS POST. SEARCH POCKETS FOR ORDERS.'

Then there were two Scots who bet a pound on who could stay underwater the longest. They both drowned.

A Scotsman started a fantastic new sweepstake with a first prize of a million pounds – £1 a year for a million years.

One day Jock bought a bottle of single-malt whisky and while walking home he fell. On getting up, he felt something wet on his kilt. He looked up at the sky and said, 'Oh Lord, please, I beg you, let it be blood.'

A Scotsman and an Englishman were having a magnificent meal at one of the best restaurants in London. At the end of the evening, the waiter came over to present the bill and a Scottish voice said, 'That's all right, laddie, just gie it to me.'

The headline in the newspaper next day proclaimed, 'Ventriloquist Found Beaten to Death'.

An Englishman, an Irishman and a Scotsman were discussing sporting events.

'The closest race I ever saw,' said the Englishman,

'was a car race, in which one of the cars had been recently painted and won by the breadth of the coat of paint.'

'The closest race I ever saw,' said the Scotsman, 'was a horse race, in which a horse, stung by a bee, won by the length of the bee sting swelling on his nose.'

'The closest race I ever saw,' said the Irishman, 'are the Scots.'

Why are Scotsmen so good at golf?

They realise that the fewer times they hit the ball the longer it will last.

Do you know why there are eighteen holes on a golf course? It's because that's how long it took the Scottish inventor of the game to finish his bottle of whisky.

Did you hear about the Scots golfer who wore a black armband? He'd lost a ball.

It is now generally accepted that golf did not originate in Scotland. No Scotsman would invent a game in which it was possible to lose a ball.

Have you heard about the lucky Scotsman?

He was always finding money under plates in restaurants.

Did you hear about the Scotsman who married a girl born on February the 29th so he'd only have to buy her a birthday present every four years?

An old Scottish proverb: No matter how much you applaud a jukebox, you have to put another coin in for an encore.

Scottish preacher to his congregation: 'I don't mind you putting buttons in the collection plate, but please provide your own buttons. Stop pulling them off the church cushions.'

'Well,' said the Englishman to the Scot, as they got off the train, 'it's been a very long and tiring journey.'
  'Yes,' said the Scot, 'and so it should be, for what the fare cost.'

The Scot rushed into the chemist shop. 'I'm needing £10 worth of your best heroin,' he announced.
  'What for?' asked the chemist suspiciously.
  '£5.'

'I hear McDougal left over five million pounds when he died,' said McNab.
  'McDougal didn't leave that money,' said McTavish. 'He was taken from it.'

A big crowd gathered on the banks of Loch Ness and watched the tourist apply artificial respiration to the Highland lassie he'd just rescued. Her parents broke through the crowds, joyful at seeing their daughter alive and well.

'Sandy,' said the happy mother, 'give that kind Englishman a pound. He saved our daughter's life.'

'But, Mum,' protested the lass, 'I was half dead.'

'All right,' Mum said, 'give him fifty pence.'

It was a great party. The Italian brought the wine. The Englishman brought roast beef. The Frenchman brought onions. The Scot brought his brother.

An Englishman was sent to Stornoway on the Isle of Lewis on a month-long contract. He arrived on a grey, cloudy rainy day. He woke up the next morning to find it was grey, cloudy and raining. The next day it was the same, and the next. On the day after that, as he came out of his room to find it was grey, cloudy and raining, he saw a small boy passing and said in exasperation, 'Does the weather ever change here?'

'I really don't know,' said the lad, 'I'm only six.'

'Ah, Fiona, drinking makes you look so bonnie.'

'But, Donald, I dinna drink.'

'I do!'

'Now, MacDonald,' said the doctor, 'it's like this. You have either to stop the whisky or lose your eyesight, and you must choose.'

'Och, well, doctor,' said old MacDonald. 'I'm a very old man now and I was thinking that I have probably seen about everything that's worth seeing.'

A Scotsman has been in the pub all night. The bartender finally says that the bar is closed. So he stands up to leave and falls flat on his face. He figures he'll crawl outside and get some fresh air and maybe that will sober him up. Once outside, he stands up and falls flat on his face. So he crawls home and at the door stands up and falls flat on his face. He crawls through the door and up the stairs. When he reaches his bed, he tries one more time to stand up. This time he falls right into bed and is sound asleep.

He awakens the next morning to his wife standing over him shouting at him. 'So, you've been out drinking again!'

'How did you know?' he asks.

'The pub called – you left your wheelchair there again.'

Donald said to his wife one night, 'Well, Maggie, I think I'll go and pay a visit to our new neighbour, the White Settler Englishman.'

On his return some time later, Maggie asked, 'Well, Donald, what kind of man is our neighbour?'

'He's a good man,' replied Donald, 'a good man and very free with the whisky. But it is very poor quality. They have no idea about whisky, the English. In fact, Maggie, it was that bad, I nearly left some.'

A Scotsman will never be insulted if you offer him a very small glass of whisky. He will merely swallow the insult.

There are two things a Scot likes naked.

One of them is malt whisky.

The other is another malt whisky.

Owed to a Haggis

Oh, what a sleekit horrible beastie
Lurks in yer belly efter the feastie
Just as ye sit doon among yer kin
There starts to stir an enormous wind.

The neeps and tatties and mushy peas
Start workin' like a gentle breeze
But soon the puddin' wi' the sonsie face
Will have ye blawin' a' oor the place.

Scotland vs England

Nae matter whit the hell ye dae
Everbody's gonnae have tae pay
Even if ye try to stifle
It's like a bullet oot a rifle.

Haud yer bum tight tae the chair
Tae try and stop the leakin' air
Shift yersel' frae cheek tae cheek
Prae tae God it disnae reek.

But aw yer efforts go asunder
Oot it comes like a clap a thunder
Ricochets aroon' the room
Michty me, a sonic boom!

God almighty, it fairly reeks;
Hope I huvnae shit ma breeks
Tae the bog I better scurry
Aw, whit the hell, it's no' ma worry.

Everybody roon' aboot me chokin'
Wan or two are nearly bokin'
I'll feel better for a while
Cannae help but raise a smile.

'Wis him!' I shout with accusin' glower
Alas too late, he's just keeled ower

'Ye dirty bugger!' they shout and stare
I dinnae feel welcome any mair.

Where ere ye go let yer wind go free
Sounds like just the job fur me
Whit a fuss at Rabbie's perty
Ower the sake ae wan wee ferty.

An eighteen-year-old Glasgow girl tells her mum that she has missed her period for two months. Very worried, the mother goes to Boots and buys a pregnancy kit. The test result shows that the girl is pregnant.

Shouting, cursing and crying, the mother says, 'Who was the pig that did this to you? I want to know!'

The girl picks up the phone and makes a call.

Her dad is saying over and over, 'Just as long as he's not English or from Edinburgh.'

Half an hour later, a Ferrari stops in front of their house. A mature and distinguished Englishman with grey hair, impeccably dressed in a very expensive suit, steps out of it and enters the house.

He sits in the living room with the father, the mother and the girl, and tells them, 'Good morning, your daughter has informed me of the problem. I can't marry her, however, because of my personal family situation, but I'll take responsibility. If a girl is born I

141

will bequeath her two big retail stores, a large house, a beach villa in a country of her choice and a £1,000,000 bank account. If a boy is born, my legacy will be a couple of factories and a £2,000,000 bank account. If it is twins, four factories and £1,000,000 each. However, if there is a miscarriage . . .'

At this point, the father, who has remained silent, places a hand firmly on the man's shoulder and says, 'You'll try again, eh?'

23
Funnily Enough, Not Everyone Likes Scotland

It requires a surgical operation to get a joke well into a Scotsman's understanding.

Sydney Smith

Oats: a grain which in England is generally given to horses, but in Scotland supports the people.

Samuel Johnson

The great thing about Glasgow now is that if there is a nuclear attack it'll look exactly the same afterwards.

Billy Connolly

Much may be made of a Scotsman, if he is caught young.

Samuel Johnson

The noblest prospect which a Scotsman ever sees, is the high road that leads him to England.

Samuel Johnson

Scotland: That garret of the earth – that knuckle-end of England – that land of Calvin, oatcakes, and sulphur.
  Sydney Smith

There are few more impressive sights in the world than a Scotsman on the make.
  James Barrie

I have been trying all my life to like Scotchmen, and am obliged to desist from the experiment in despair.
  Charles Lamb

If the Scotch knew enough to go in when it rained, they would never get any outdoor exercise.
  Simeon Ford

In all my travels I never met with any one Scotchman but what was a man of sense. I believe everybody of that country that has any, leaves it as fast as they can.
  Francis Lockier

It is never difficult to distinguish between a Scotsman with a grievance and a ray of sunshine.
  Sir Pelham Grenville Wodehouse

The Scots invented golf – which could also explain why they invented Scotch.

James Dent

And three by Anonymous:

In Scotland, you're considered posh if you have slates on your roof. Indeed, if you have a roof.

If you take a picture of a Scotsman, he runs about claiming you stole his soul.

I wish Scotland would snap off and sink!

24
Anthems

Tear to a Glass Eye Time

God grant that Marshall Wade,
May by thy mighty aid,
victory bring.
May he sedition hush,
and like a torrent rush,
Rebellious Scots to crush,
God save the King.

This is verse six of 'God Save the King/Queen'. Traditionally, the first performance of this verse was thought to have been in 1745, when it was sung in support of George II after the defeat of his army at the Battle of Prestonpans by Charles Edward Stuart, the bonnie prince, whose forces were mostly Scottish.

Land of Hope and Glory, Mother of the Free,
How shall we extol thee, who are born of thee?

Wider still, and wider, shall thy bounds be set;
God, who made thee mighty, make thee mightier yet!

Anthems

Truth and Right and Freedom, each a holy gem,
Stars of solemn brightness, weave thy diadem.

Tho' thy way be darkened, still in splendour drest,
As the star that trembles o'er the liquid West.

Throned amid the billows, throned inviolate,
Thou hast reigned victorious, thou has smiled at fate.

Land of Hope and Glory, fortress of the Free,
How may we extol thee, praise thee, honour thee?

Hark, a mighty nation maketh glad reply;
Lo, our lips are thankful, lo, our hearts are high!

Hearts in hope uplifted, loyal lips that sing;
Strong in faith and freedom, we have crowned our
King!

The words are by Arthur C. Benson (1862–1925), who wrote them in close collaboration with the composer Edward Elgar (1857–1934). In 1901 Elgar produced the first two of his five 'Pomp and Circumstance' marches and it is the central theme of his 'Pomp and Circumstance March No. 1' in D that provides the superb tune to these words. Elgar wrote some really great tunes and he always knew when he was on to a winner. About this one he wrote at the time to a friend, 'I've got a tune that will knock 'em – knock 'em flat!'

He was right. And the tune was so much appreciated by Edward VII that Elgar was commissioned to compose a work for the coronation of the king, later to be known as the 'Coronation Ode'. The tune was incorporated into this Ode, and this resulted in the song 'Land of Hope and Glory'. The 'Coronation Ode' was finished in April 1902 and assured Elgar of a knighthood, in 1904. The Ode was also performed at the coronation of King George V in 1911.

I was sent the above by an English chap, Steve Ellis, from my pub, who got it, he thinks, from a BBC website – or an EBC website, as it is known in this household – so thanks to them, perhaps. And, if they sue, it is down to you, Stevo.

25
First Foot Is Not Just for Hogmanay

FirstFoot.com is a Glasgow-based site of eternal pristine irreverence, occasional seat-wetting humour and sometimes rock-solid good sense. This is their Q&A introduction, used with their permission. Scots and Sassenachs both might find something that they like there.

Who are the people behind FirstFoot?
We are, obviously.

Can you be a bit more specific?
Oh all right then.

We are two simple Scottish patriots who believe in freedom of speech and the honest, warts and all portrayal of our country beyond the sanitised shortbread-tin image so beloved of our tourist industry and most other Scottish websites.

Why is the Scottish International football team so shite?
So as not to distract attention from how superb the Scottish supporters are.

Why do the Scots hate the English?

We could give you all that historical guff about being invaded and interfered with for centuries before finally being swallowed whole against the democratic wishes of the Scottish people, but the real truth in a civilised 21st-century Scotland is that we don't hate the English at all. We just pretend to because we know it annoys them so much.

What is tossing the caber all about?

People are often curious to know why men in the Highlands use tree trunks to pick up and throw high into the air, for no apparent reason other than to see how it lands. The answer is simple. In the Highlands, there is never an Englishman lying about when you want one so trees have to suffice.

The best caber tossers tend to be physically very big and Scotland has no lack of champions in this particular sport. Indeed, some of the biggest tossers in the world are Scottish.

The sport has also been exported to many countries with large ex-pat communities and Canada in particular is full of tossers.

Why do the Scots never support England?

There are two answers to this:

If you are reading this and you are English, it's

because you are arrogant, imperialist, insensitive, ugly, stupid, money-grabbing bastards.

If you are not English, we do it because it annoys the fuck out of them and they can't wrap their heads round it (due mainly to in-breeding because no other nation wants to shag them).

Why are the Scottish football fans so well behaved in comparison to England's?

Because we don't drink, don't smoke, don't swear and we go to church every Sunday. And we have parents who are married.

How come a big mush of rotting cereal and stuff mixed with boggy water and left to fester can become the world's most popular drink?

Advertising and Prohibition – but not in that order.

What's all this Catholic vs Protestant rivalry stuff in the West of Scotland about?

Nae idea. Read the Bible for clues.

We think it might be something to do with football though.

Why did they build Edinburgh Castle so far from the shops in Princes Street?

For the same reason they didn't build an escalator up to the esplanade, you stupid American twat.

Was William Wallace really Australian, like in the film?

No. He came from near Paisley, which is just as awful.

Why were the Bay City Rollers?

This is one of those imponderable questions that can't really be answered – like why does influenza exist? Like every one of their songs, there is absolutely no rhyme or reason to it. The Rollers were something of an accident that just happened without any real justification and we're very, very sorry and would like to apologise profusely to the world on behalf of the Scottish nation with our promise that it will never, ever be allowed to happen again.

What does a deep-fried Mars Bar taste like?

Shite.

Why does whisky get you drunk?

In order to stimulate sales of Barr's Irn-Bru, the world's finest hangover cure.

Do Scotsmen wear anything under a kilt?

Only if they have very small penises.

What does haggis taste like?

Shite.

Why do Scots people drink so much?

To forget . . . something . . .

What is the ugliest town in Scotland?

Without question, it has to be Cowdenbeath. Apologies to all you peoploids with a soft spot for Cowdenbeath, but it is a complete shithole.

What is the ugliest village in Scotland?

Difficult but FirstFoot prefers Fallin, near Stirling. Once again, apologies to the good people of Fallin, but it is a mingin' slagheap.

What are the ingredients of a haggis?

    Coarse sand
    Curry sauce from Tony's Chippy in Barrhead
    Three-day-old mince
    Desiccated Black Jacks
    All stuffed inside a burst plastic football
    Yum!

Do Scotsmen make good lovers?

Most Scots men can maintain an erection all night. However, they may be asleep for most of this time.

Are midgies really a nuisance?

Does Dolly Parton sleep on her back?

Midgies are right annoying wee bastards.

Why do Scots use so much brown sauce?

Because the food tastes bloody awful without it.

Are all Scots men called Jimmy?

No. Some Scots men are also called Ken.

In these instances, sentences like 'Ah'm doolally, Jimmy, ken!' can be confusing.

The above sentence means 'My friend, I am vertically challenged due to over indulgence in alcohol. Have you experienced this before?'

Do Scotswomen make good lovers?

Yes.

Many Scots women will consent to making love before consuming vast quantities of alcohol and/or drugs.

Is there a European standard for Sporrans?

Yes. Under article 34523 of European law, a sporran must be able to hold:

Twelve cans of lager

Twenty Embassy Regal

£235 in coins

Passport

Match tickets

Mobile phone

Half bottle of whisky

And a fish supper.

26

A List of All of the Benefits that Have Accrued to Scotland from the Acts of Union

PTO

Benefits that Have Accrued to Scotland from the Acts of Union

PTO

Scotland vs England

PTO

Benefits that Have Accrued to Scotland from the Acts of Union

PTO

Scotland vs England

PTO

Benefits that Have Accrued to Scotland from the Acts of Union

PTO

Scotland vs England

PTO

Benefits that Have Accrued to Scotland from the Acts of Union

PTO

Scotland vs England

PTO

Benefits that Have Accrued to Scotland from the Acts of Union

PTO

Scotland vs England

PTO

Benefits that Have Accrued to Scotland from the Acts of Union

PTO

Naw, me neither.